The Learning Leader

REFLECTING, MODELING, AND SHARING

Jacqueline E. Jacobs

Kevin L. O'Gorman

Routledge
Taylor & Francis Group
New York London

First published 2012 by Eye On Education

Published 2013 by Routledge
711 Third Avenue, New York, NY 10017, USA
2 Park Square, Milton Park, Abingdon, Oxon OX14 4RN

Routledge is an imprint of the Taylor & Francis Group, an informa business

Library of Congress Cataloging-in-Publication Data

Jacobs, Jacqueline E., 1947–
The learning leader : reflecting, modeling, and sharing / Jacqueline E. Jacobs, Ph.D., Kevin L. O'Gorman, Ph.D.
pages cm
Includes bibliographical references.
ISBN 978-1-59667-216-1
1. School principals—In-service training. 2. Educational leadership.
I. O'Gorman, Kevin L. II. Title.
LB2831.9.J33 2012
371.2'012—dc23

2011052059

ISBN: 978-1-596-67216-1 (pbk)

Cover Designer: Dave Strauss, 3FoldDesign

Also Available from Eye On Education

The Principal's Guide to the First 100 Days of the School Year: Creating Instructional Momentum
Shawn Joseph

Lead On! Motivational Lessons for School Leaders
Pete Hall

What Great Principals Do Differently: 18 Things That Matter Most (Second Edition)
Todd Whitaker

The Fearless School Leader: Making the Right Decisions
Cynthia McCabe

Communicate and Collaborate: The School Leader's Guide to Effective Communication
Shelly Arneson

Leading School Change: 9 Strategies to Bring Everybody On Board
Todd Whitaker

Motivating and Inspiring Teachers: The Educational Leader's Guide for Building Staff Morale (Second edition)
Todd Whitaker, Beth Whitaker, & Dale Lumpa

Creating School Cultures That Embrace Learning: What Successful Leaders Do
Tony Thacker, John S. Bell, & Franklin P. Schargel

The Principalship from A to Z
Ronald Williamson & Barbara R. Blackburn

Dedication

This book is dedicated to all the fine educators in this country who, day by day, work hard to create environments that encourage students to actively engage in learning.

About the Authors

Jacqueline E. Jacobs, PhD, has served as a teacher, assistant principal, principal, director of special education, professor of special education, and professor of educational leadership on five continents. She counts among her greatest learning opportunities her interactions with students, teachers, and parents. As President of KMH Educational Consulting, LLC, she currently provides consulting to school districts on principal leadership and special education.

Kevin L. O'Gorman, PhD, is currently the Associate Superintendent for Instruction and Accountability for Aiken County Public Schools in Aiken, South Carolina. He has served as a teacher and an administrator in predominately high-poverty schools in South Carolina and has taught graduate courses in educational administration at both the University of South Carolina and Western Carolina University.

Acknowledgements

Every person is an amalgamation of personal experiences, education, and interactions with others. We, the authors, acknowledge that many people have contributed to our knowledge and experiences, which have helped to shape us personally and professionally. To each and every one, we say thank you.

Specifically, we acknowledge the following:

- Bob Sickles, for his belief that this project had merit
- Lauren Beebe, for her support and ideas as an amazing editor
- Dr. Diane Harwell, Clinical Professor, University of South Carolina
- Dr. Beth Everitt, Superintendent, Aiken County Schools
- The School Board members of Aiken County
- The Superintendent's Cabinet of Aiken County Schools
- The principals of Aiken County
- Our professional colleagues at the University of South Carolina and Western Carolina University
- All the teachers and administrators with whom we have had the privilege to serve
- And, most importantly, all the students we've had the privilege to serve

Jacque acknowledges the support and encouragement of her children, Amy, Bonnie, and Cheri, their spouses/significant others, and her grandchildren, who have inspired her. She also thanks friends, colleagues, and students who have encouraged her in this project. She is grateful to her parents, Mary Anderson Evans and Dick Evans, and her late husband, Dr. John F. Jacobs, for their never-ending belief in her.

Kevin acknowledges the support and encouragement of his wife, Liz, and the inspiration of his children, Kellsey, Olivia, and Gillian. He also thanks his parents, Louie and Gail, for teaching him the value of education.

Contents

Introduction

No matter where a school leader is in the leadership journey, from the novice to the most experienced, there will always be new things to learn and new challenges to address. Continuous learning and growth present their own challenges for leadership as do new ideas, new knowledge about teaching and learning, as well as the ever-present standards, mandates, and policies that are imposed by district, state, and national groups and lawmakers.

As a leader, you can grow only if you are willing to do so. The purpose of this book is to help you consider how you both manage and lead from your current position and how you might want to reconsider the role and responsibilities you have and assume.

While most readers may know that the principal was originally the lead teacher or "principal teacher," many people do not know this and have the view, over the last half of the twentieth century, of the principal only as manager. Principals must be the leaders of learning. They must be willing to examine their own beliefs and actions, work with teachers to examine theirs, and understand what is involved in being a leader of learning.

Mission and Vision Statements

Most state standards for school leaders include a statement on the ability to articulate a vision for the school or district. With a history, particularly over the last two decades, of writing mission statements, school leaders, generally working with school improvement councils, spend a great deal of time developing and posting these mission statements. In 2007, a group of faculty at Western Carolina University set out to do the same. During that process, one colleague said, "Let's look at what Guy Kawasaki has to say about mission statements." After viewing his video (Kawasaki, 2007), the faculty, using the brainstorming they had done on what they believe about leadership, quickly put together the following mantra: *Live Your Leadership Journey Courageously* © (Buskey, 2010). They and their students came to realize that the mantra is easily remembered, has meaning in each word, and is a guide for their beliefs and actions.

Do you use your vision or mission statement? Or does it just grace your walls?

This book is not about making the principal the guru of professional learning (the term is used synonymously with professional development) for a school, except in the context of working with others to determine needs and ensuring that the professional learning is provided, implemented, and integrated into the daily learning environment for students. The book is about leading learning of self, teachers, and students.

The ultimate recipients of the educational capacity of our schools are, of course, the students served. They, in turn, benefit the society at large through their contributions, generally as adults, to the arts, education, sciences, business, government, social service, and so on. However, in order to have an overall perspective on the importance of building capacity in students, there has to be an overriding belief on the part of school leaders, regardless of their roles (i.e., principal, director, assistant superintendent, district superintendent), that capacity must first be developed in the adults within the school environment—capacity to teach, assess learning, and lead change.

Leading Learning Requires Change

One day, as a principal, Jacque walked into the media center where the media specialist and her assistant were working their way through what seemed to be the endless task of bar coding all the books in the media center. The media specialist said, "You know, I've finally accepted that the only constant in this district is change." Thinking for a minute about what she had said, Jacque realized how often educators are prone to responding to calls for "change" with little consideration for how to lead that change.

Sometimes a well-intentioned effort to lead learning can fall short if all stakeholders are not considered. For instance, a superintendent in a large district was known for the "sweeping changes" that had occurred in that district. There was lots of media coverage of the changes. For example, his first major initiative was to offer financial support in the form of tuition reimbursement to administrators who pursued their doctorates. This was hailed as a "strong commitment" to improving the leadership of the district. Once the newspapers and television anchors had put a seal of approval on the story, the initiative had its day in the press. What never made the press was that the superintendent had not worked with anyone in his district to determine the intended outcomes of the initiative, the criteria that would be applied to the selection of the recipients who would receive support, and the obligations of the recipients to the district. The initiative became a huge boondoggle for the superintendent because he picked the initial recipients based solely on his judgment (his right, of course); they became known as the "super's favorites" group and were shunned by their peers. His stated intent to improve learning for students in his district by improving learning for his administrators was undoubtedly laudable, but the execution left much to be desired.

Reflecting . . .

> A report from the federal government (Goertz, Floden, & O'Day, 1995) suggests that the debates over building capacity for educational reform "often fail to consider the many factors that interact to determine educational capacity" (para. 2).
>
> - What do you consider the most important factors in determining educational capacity?
> - Have you identified the focus for educational capacity?
> - Is that focus on the adults (teachers, staff, administrators)?
> - Is that focus on community (local, state, national) demands?
> - Is that focus on the students you serve?
> - That is, what is your capacity to educate the students you serve?
>
> While considering the focus of educational capacity in your environment, you might also ask yourself this question: Who benefits from the education offered in your district in the short term? in the long term?

With more than a century of focusing education on teacher performance, it is hard to shift that thinking to focus on learning. But until educators have a view of learning as something that they all do, the learning of K–12 students will continue to be affected by the perception that the teacher's actions, which have changed little in a hundred years, are more important than the outcome of those actions: the student's learning. Likewise, most teachers will not learn how to change the learning environment if there is little or no expectation for learning on the part of everyone involved in a school.

So the authors welcome you to consider the ideas presented in this book. Challenge your thinking with these ideas and challenge ours. We want to grow in our thinking, and we write this book on the assumption that you do, too.

USING WHAT YOU'VE LEARNED

At the end of each chapter, you will find suggestions that will help you put what you've learned in the chapter to use.

In your calendar, make a note on the date of the next principals' meeting to ask three or four principals these two questions:

1. What is the origin of the word *principal*?
2. What do you do to lead learning in your school?

Their responses will help you to examine your own ideas and beliefs and decide if you really think the principal can be the *principal teacher* who is responsible for leading learning for self, teachers, and students.

1

Learning in the Twenty-First Century: What Is the Literature Telling Us?

Over time, educators have created a lexicon of buzzwords that any etymologist would be proud to study. Similar to the dialect of a teenage clique, teacher jargon confuses the outsider (and often the insider) and changes so rapidly that those who do not use the language daily can get lost over time. Words like *rigor* and *engaged*, concepts like *high expectations* and *disabled* are thrown around by educators as if everyone had a clear and agreed-upon understanding of their exact meaning. Educators hear these terms being used by peers and, in order to remain part of the club and to sound as though we know what we are talking about, we sling the same terms around. Typically, the sad reality of the education world is that teachers easily use new vocabulary, but they are not talking about anything new.

The notion of twenty-first-century learning is not necessarily a breakthrough in the evolutionary process of K–12 education, but it does remind

Reflecting . . .

> *Critical thinking* is one of the buzzwords (or phrases) associated with twenty-first-century learning. It has been defined as "self-directed, self-disciplined, self-monitored, and self-corrective thinking" (Critical Thinking Community, 2010). Collaboration with others in order to solve problems is also considered a twenty-first-century learning skill. Interestingly enough, Plato and Xenophon created examples of the Socratic method, obviously named for Socrates, in Socratic dialogues around 400 BCE.
>
> Is twenty-first-century learning something new, or has it just taken educators until the year 2011 to realize that they failed to incorporate the foundational and fundamental practices for *thinking* and learning that Socrates and Plato tried to teach so long ago?

us of our philosophical roots in the art of teaching. The importance of this emerging concept is that it points out some foundational practices that appear to have escaped the education world over the past 2,400 years and applies those practices to the skills needed in the modern workplace.

After many years in education, Kevin readily admits his father was right. Readers no doubt can empathize with how difficult that can be to say. His father, a longtime educator in public schools, used to lecture all his high-school-age children that "the problem with the education you are receiving is that it does not include classes in philosophy." No one was teaching Kevin and his siblings how to *think* about the content they were learning. The Socratic method, for example, was not a strategy that they were taught in high school—and it is not being taught in most public schools currently. Today, we will take Kevin's father's concern about the lack of philosophy in the schools a step further. As educators, our initial charge should be that we are to teach our students how to *think,* and then we should use content (English, math, science, social studies, the arts, etc.) as a venue through which to teach thinking. In order to make that cultural shift, educators will have to retreat from an educational philosophy that shaped the current system more than 120 years ago and engage themselves in twenty-first-century learning.

Sharing Perspectives On Twenty-First-Century Learning

Think about trying twenty-first-century learning so you can model examples for teachers and colleagues:

Before reading any further, do some of your own research regarding twenty-first-century learning, call some colleagues and ask them about their understanding of the concept, develop your own conclusions, read our findings below with a critical eye, and then log your own definition. This process makes the definition *yours*—and you do not depend on anyone else to give you *the* answer.

There was a time when "one right answer" or a lockstep philosophy was appropriate, but twenty-first-century learning calls for more flexibility and imagination. Think about how your students might take ownership of their own learning when provided with this same type of opportunity in your classrooms. Think about how long they will remember that definition as opposed to memorizing one provided to them by the teacher or read in a textbook.

Then take these recommendations and turn them into a professional development activity for your teachers. Engage them in developing a definition for twenty-first-century learning in your own school.

Reflecting . . .

> As you read through the rest of this chapter and learn more about the skills associated with twenty-first-century learning, think about the educators you know and ask yourself if they are using those twenty-first-century learning skills to develop lesson plans, create assessments, analyze student achievement data, choose curricula, and so on. If your answer is no, then think about how you can model those skills in order to have them replicated in your schools.

Defining Twenty-First-Century Learning

If schools aren't teaching twenty-first-century learning skills now, then what century's skills are they teaching? Heidi Jacobs (2010) discusses the ramifications of the National Education Association's Committee of Ten. In 1892, it was appointed to study and make curriculum recommendations, taking into consideration the Industrial Revolution. The committee recommended that all students be taught the same curriculum, regardless of their academic prowess. In addition, the committee recommended that schools be developed like factories, where students attend school for eight hours a day, 180 days a year; that a student's education would last twelve years; and that the purpose of elementary schools was to prepare students for the curriculum at the high-school level. Interestingly enough, various groups at this time debated whether students should memorize pertinent content information of the time, acquire critical thinking skills, and/or undertake Latin and Greek studies. If the reader is a current educator, then the answer to how this debate finished is clear. Please know that the authors are not suggesting that everything taught in public schools today based on the recommendations of the Committee of Ten is all bad or that the mandates enforced in 1892 were inappropriate for the time. Rather, we suggest that our public schools currently have only part of the equation right—and they are well past the due date for a change.

Much as the Industrial Revolution inspired awareness that the educational system needed a major overhaul in the late 1800s, there is a technological revolution today that calls for an equivalent change. Technology today has two characteristics that should create a sense of urgency in educators to call for change. First, and foremost, technology is shrinking the globe. Citizens of the United States and of almost every other country are interacting within virtual communities every day. Teachers *must* prepare their students to be ready to compete in a global market. The second characteristic of technology that calls for immediate attention is its ever-changing state. Because the transformations of technology shift both the speed at which people can communicate with each other and the mode in which they communicate with each other, future generations will have to be able to adapt to a rapidly changing world environment.

Tony Wagner's *The Global Achievement Gap* (2008) communicates an inspiring vision for twenty-first-century learning. Wagner's work is referenced numerous times on Internet sites and in books that pop up among the 23 million hits on a Google search for "twenty-first-century learning." A video interview of Wagner, located at SchoolChange.org (Wagner, 2010), reveals valuable insight into the skills students will need in college and their careers and what educators need to do in order to meet those needs.

During the interview and in his book, Wagner focuses on the changes in work, learning, and citizenship in the United States. He discusses the changes in the workplace as factory positions move to other countries. His description of the change in the types of jobs prevalent in the United States clearly denotes that the findings of the Committee of Ten are obsolete. So, if schools shouldn't operate like factories or prepare students to work in factories, then how should they operate, and what are students supposed to be learning?

Below are seven skills for twenty-first-century learning that Wagner references, with a short description or explanation of each, that K–12 students and adults need to acquire in order to be successful in the twenty-first century:

1. **Critical Thinking and Problem Solving**

   Reason effectively:

   - Use various types of reasoning (inductive, deductive, etc.) as appropriate to the situation

   Use systems thinking:

   - Analyze how parts of a whole interact with each other to produce overall outcomes in complex systems

   Make judgments and decisions:

   - Effectively analyze and evaluate evidence, arguments, claims, and beliefs
   - Analyze and evaluate major alternative points of view
   - Synthesize and make connections between information and arguments

- Interpret information and draw conclusions based on the best analysis
- Reflect critically on learning experiences and processes

Solve problems:

- Solve different kinds of unfamiliar problems in both conventional and innovative ways
- Identify and ask significant questions that clarify various points of view and lead to better solutions (Partnership for 21st Century Learning Skills, 2010)

2. **Collaboration Across Networks and Leading by Influence**

   In order to be effective citizens and to achieve common goals in a democracy, adults and students alike need to be able to exert their influence and leadership skills on diverse groups of people in their respective communities (Wagner, 2010).

3. **Agility and Adaptability**

   Adults and students need to learn to adapt to an ever-changing work environment in order to be successful in the future.

4. **Initiative and Entrepreneurialism**

   Manage goals and time:

   - Set goals with tangible and intangible success criteria
   - Balance tactical (short-term) and strategic (long-term) goals
   - Utilize time and manage workload efficiently
   - Work independently
   - Monitor, define, prioritize, and complete tasks without direct oversight

   Be self-directed learners:

   - Go beyond basic mastery of skills and/or curriculum to explore and expand one's own learning and opportunities to gain expertise
   - Demonstrate initiative to advance skill levels toward a professional level
   - Demonstrate commitment to learning as a lifelong process
   - Reflect critically on past experiences in order to inform future progress (Partnership for 21st Century Skills, 2010)

5. **Effective Oral and Written Communication**

   Students and teachers alike need to be able to communicate with diverse groups of people both orally and in written form. This includes the use of digital forms of communication such as e-mails, text messages, blogs, wikis, and so on.

6. **Accessing and Analyzing Information**

   Students and teachers need to be able to understand how to access information, filter good information from bad through effective analysis practices, and synthesize information into something meaningful to achieve specific goals.

7. **Curiosity and Imagination**

   "Think outside the box" has become an all-too-familiar phrase that only scratches the surface of what Wagner is trying to communicate about incorporating curiosity and imagination into what educators should try to accomplish. Part of the problem educators face, usually unknowingly, is that they aren't even sure of the parameters of their own boxes—so thinking outside the box is a stab in the dark at best. Educators need to understand the current limitations of what they're trying to accomplish before they can begin to expand those boundaries. Learning how to create completely fluid boundaries for student learning while maintaining a framework for making instructional decisions is the teacher's ultimate goal. Educators need to give themselves permission to allow their imaginations to drive their classrooms—and in turn to allow curiosity and imagination to drive the learning of students as opposed to being anchored down by their preconceived notions of what "school" is supposed to be.

Which of these seven skills might you see in a factory line? How many of these skills are currently being taught in your classrooms? How many of these skills do you use or do your teachers use to develop lesson plans or school improvement plans?

Utilizing and implementing the seven skills listed previously into K–12 schools will not be accomplished for students if those same concepts are not applied to professional development for educators. Every educator needs to be able to work in a team in order to make the transition from traditional schooling to twenty-first-century learning. Wagner points out that educa-

Reflecting . . .

> "Empty your mind, be formless, shapeless—like water. Now you put water into a cup, it becomes the cup, you put water into a bottle, it becomes the bottle, you put it in a teapot, it becomes the teapot. Now water can flow or it can crash. Be water, my friend" (Bruce Lee, 1971).

tors, for the most part, are not ready to work on teams because they crave autonomy. Most teachers are familiar with colleagues who come to school every day, shut the door to their classrooms, teach their lessons, and then go home with little or no interaction with other adults. This kind of isolation is the enemy of modern schools. If your teachers are not willing to work in teams, then how can you expect them to teach students to work on teams?

In *The Global Achievement Gap*, Wagner also discusses testing as an area that needs to be drastically improved. In short, the problem with current assessments is that they do not assess what teachers are trying to accomplish! Current tests are not designed to provide information about how successful students will be in college or the workplace or if they will be able to compete in the global market. Much like a road test for a driver's license, K–12 assessments should reflect real-life situations for students.

Think about the dilemma that the astronauts and flight administrators faced during the flight of *Apollo 13*. At one point during the mission, the astronauts were running out of oxygen and, because of an electrical malfunction, they did not have the right connection piece to get oxygen from the oxygen tank into their craft. The folks at Houston were charged with designing a connector using only the tools and materials that the astronauts had on board at the time. That was a real test—with many possible solutions! Most real-life problems don't have just one right solution—but K–12 assessments usually do. The only way educators can know if students are prepared for college and the workplace is to assess them in real-life situations.

The mere introduction of the term *twenty-first-century learning* into the world of education acknowledges that current students are living in the twenty-first century, but today's instructional practices are not in sync with the modern age or the real world. Educators should be ahead of the curve in understanding what their students need in order to be successful in the workplace or in college, but, sadly enough, today educators are well behind the curve! Some of the definitions of twenty-first-century learning suggest that educators be proactive by incorporating teaching processes that will help students adapt to an ever-changing world.

When researching twenty-first-century learning, you may not find consistency in its definition. However, most of the descriptions of twenty-first-century learning require a process that, when implemented, would break some of the rote instructional practices recommended by the Committee of Ten. Because of the various ways current writers discuss this concept, the authors encourage educators to share their thoughts about twenty-first-century learning on different fronts: technology, instruction, professional development, and leadership. The availability and widespread use of technology demands instructional practices that provide more appropriate learning goals for students, goals that can be attained only through good professional development facilitated by skilled instructional leaders.

Technology Calls for Action

According to Kreis (2000), two factors accelerated the spread of the Renaissance—a prosperous economy and the printing press. If the printing press had such an effect on the Renaissance, how does the Internet affect today's educational system? According to the nineteenth-century historian Thomas Carlyle, "He who first shortened the labor of copyists by device of movable types was disbanding hired armies, and cashiering most kings and senates, and creating a whole new democratic world: he had invented the art of printing" ([1833]2000). A modern-day parallel, specific to education and technology, might read something like this: The students who reach out to the world through technology defy the constraints of today's public education and leap beyond the boundaries of their classrooms and their countries—without direction from their educators; they are the genesis of virtual world communities that claim no nationality, answer to no authority, and are established by no historical template. So who are the students reaching out to the world through technology?

Contemporary writers often refer to students currently in K–12 schools as the "net generation." Cultural generations typically refer to cohorts of people similar in age that have experienced the same shift in culture caused by industrialization, modernization, westernization, and so on. Today's technology has created a new generation, no doubt, but is it only one generation? Kevin has one daughter who is seventeen and one who is two, and they clearly belong to two separate generations in terms of how their lives and their respective cultures will be influenced by technology. His high-school daughter writes her homework papers on the computer, prints them, and then turns them in to be graded by hand. His younger daughter is not likely to go through that experience. Chances are, she will submit all her assignments online, they will be developed in collaboration with her peers, and the topics on which she writes will be more independently chosen.

When Kevin's eldest daughter was born, e-mail was still relatively new and MP3s were nonexistent. His two-year-old already knows how to turn on "tunes" on a laptop—and the current technology director for a local school district believes that e-mail will be replaced by something more efficient (morphed wikis, blogs, tweets, for example) in just a few years. Video chat is currently available as a free tool from various software companies. Is it possible to even begin to predict how that will change our culture in the next ten years?

Technology is certainly changing the way children, and students, interact with each other and the rest of the world around them—and it may very well be the cure for apathy that so many teachers appear to be seeking. There are two complaints heard consistently from principals and teachers. The first is that there is not enough time to do what needs to be done in a day, a lament that isn't unique to education. The second most popular complaint is that students and parents don't care about school or education. George Carlin once used the joke, "The government announced last week that they had discovered a cure for apathy . . . but no one seemed to care." Is it possible that educators know the solution to the apathetic attitudes of their students, but refuse to act on it?

The authors submit that the reader of this book currently knows what it is going to take to engage students in school and to cure student apathy—right now! Teachers complain all the time that students do not care about school, but in almost the same breath they identify what students *do* care about: students want only to "watch TV, play on the computer, and listen to their headphones." Instead of expecting students to enjoy and participate in the classroom activities that are developed for them that do not engage them, why don't educators simply use the activities that they *already know* engage students and build in the content they want students to learn? Is it because educators have too much pride to admit that they need to learn more about what their students enjoy? Are teachers so set in their own ways of thinking how education should "look" that they refuse to consider changing that picture—although the needs of their students clearly call for a change? Is it possible that change does not have to be drastic to begin with?

Typically, when people try to picture what twenty-first-century schools will look like, they see classrooms (organized much like the classrooms they sat in) full of computers, monitors, interactive whiteboards, hand-held devices, and other electronic equipment. While it is true that the tools used as this new century progresses will differ from even the tools currently being used, that is not the only difference. Given the fast pace of technology, newly invented computers and other technological instruments become obsolete in just a few years. How can schools keep up with the changing pace in terms of physical space?

Twenty-First-Century Classroom Setup

Describing fifteen education trends that impact school planning, Kenneth Stevenson (2010, p. 9) suggests that "technology is advancing at such a rapid rate that it is nearly impossible to plan school structures that remain 'cutting-edge' for very long after opening. However, schools planned with the greatest flexibility in terms of adding (and removing) technology will best support continuously emerging technology-based instructional methodologies and operational management approaches." This is certainly true at the classroom level as well. Teachers need to understand that their incorporation of technology needs to be versatile—and constantly upgraded. This includes both the strategies and the hardware.

Teachers often discuss their "need" for certain technological devices, such as interactive whiteboards, but most teachers use the whiteboard merely as a screen. They aren't using the software at all. When making a decision about purchasing technology, educators need to think about the purpose of that technology as well as how its impact on student achievement is going to be monitored and evaluated. And, equally important, teachers need adequate time to learn how to use the technology themselves in order to ensure meaningful learning for students.

However, twenty-first-century classrooms aren't simply about adding technology; they should be organized to enhance the seven traits Wagner suggested. Robert Beichner (2010) developed a model for a classroom set-up that promotes active and collaborative learning called Student-Centered Active Learning Environment for Undergraduate Programs (SCALE UP). Below is a short description of the model, which is provided on the SCALE UP frequently-asked-questions web page:

> The basic idea is that you give students something interesting to investigate. While they work in teams, the instructor is free to roam around the classroom—asking questions, sending one team to help another, or asking why someone else got a different answer. There is no separate lab class and most of the "lectures" are actually class-wide discussions. We carefully structure the groups and give them

> many opportunities to interact. Three teams (named a, b, and c) sit at a round table and have whiteboards nearby. Each team has a laptop in case they need web access. At North Carolina State University (the original site), classes usually have 11 tables of nine students, but many schools have smaller classes while a few have even larger ones. (Beichner, 2010, para. 2)

Although this description refers to technology, the main idea is how students interact during instruction and how the teacher acts as facilitator. The process described for organizing a classroom isn't dependent upon the type of technology that is being used by students or teachers—it's based on the need for interaction among students. Is there any reason this model couldn't be replicated in a high school or middle school? Although technology is a driving factor in changing the culture and interests of students, the way teachers teach can remain consistent no matter what technology is available.

Instruction (Teaching and Learning)

A comedian once discussed how the directions on a shampoo bottle confused him because he was not sure when he should quit washing. The directions read, "Wet hair, lather in shampoo, rinse, *repeat*; wet hair, lather in shampoo, rinse, *repeat*; wet hair, lather in shampoo, rinse, *repeat* . . ." For more than 120 years, educators have continued to educate students through rote means, and some students learn and some do not, *repeat*. Paradoxically, educators are taught according to the same philosophy. What is keeping us from changing that repetition? Until we begin teaching critical thinking skills to our students (who include our future teachers), we will not develop educators that have those skills.

Perhaps it is easiest to start a description of what instruction in a twenty-first-century classroom should look like through a nonexample. Imagine a high-school classroom in which a foreign-language teacher is reviewing exam answers that most of the class got wrong. She types the answers on a laptop at her podium in front of the class; the answers are projected through a ceiling-mounted LCD projector onto an interactive whiteboard. The students, sitting at individual desks in straight rows facing the front of the class, watch and listen while the teacher discusses the exam. That is, some of the students watch and listen; others are reading books for other classes, reading books for pleasure, sleeping, or daydreaming. Imagine those students' responses if they were asked, "What happened during that lesson? Was it teacher correcting or student learning? Who was actually 'doing' something?"

Most of us sat in similar classrooms. The only difference in teaching practices between this classroom and the one that Laura Ingalls Wilder attended is that this teacher uses a laptop and interactive whiteboard instead of chalk and a blackboard (note, however, that the whiteboard is being used merely as a screen). Even if each student had a laptop or other personal technology device, we would still have to change a few things in order to make this a completely different environment from the schools of a hundred years ago.

Most teachers can empathize with the apparent apathy plaguing this teacher's classroom. The most disturbing (though not surprising) part of this scenario, which occurred during a classroom observation, was that after the lesson, the teacher said, "You see what I have to deal with every day?" The implication was that she thought *someone else* needed to teach her students to understand the value of what they were learning and that their faulty attitudes kept them from participating in the lesson. So—why don't the students see any value in the lesson? Is it because they simply don't care about learning? Or is it that their minds are engaged in something more interesting than what the teacher has to say?

Let us digress for a moment and consider the concept of engagement. Think about the best movie you ever saw, the most exciting sports game you ever witnessed, your favorite song, your favorite book, the tastiest meal you ever ate—or even getting a cavity filled! Now compare any one of those thoughts to sitting in a typical classroom. What's the difference? Clearly the level of engagement in an activity ties both our memory and attitude to the activity, but we also place our own internal value on activities based on our level of engagement. Actors and professional sports players make more money than teachers and the president because, as a society, we value the entertainment they provide because they engage us in a positive experience. We dislike paying taxes, getting a cavity filled, standing in long lines, and sitting in some classrooms because they do not engage us in a positive experience—and they keep us from the experiences in which we want to engage (and, for that, we remember severely negative experiences as well)! We all look forward to activities that positively engage us, whether it is going out to eat with friends or sitting on the couch on a rainy day reading a good book. Do we subconsciously set our own value on activities or material objects based on our level of engagement in those activities?

Let's go back to the discussion on apathy. Note that the complaint from teachers is that students and parents do not value school or education—not that they don't care about *learning*. Kevin once had the opportunity to talk with some gang members from the neighborhood adjacent to the school in which he was principal at the time. For several weeks he noticed new gang symbols spray-painted on the school walls each Monday morning (gangs were announcing their arrival!). They played the cat-and-mouse game for a while: gang members would paint their symbols on the walls and the janitor would clean them off, *repeat*. After discussing the matter with local law enforcement, Kevin became intrigued with the culture of the gangs. He spoke to some of his students, who openly discussed the rules of their gang, what certain symbols meant, how the hierarchy worked (they didn't know that this word described what they were telling him, but he used the opportunity to teach them that). The number of rules and facts students had to memorize amazed him! They could recite, from memory, *pages* of history about their gangs, rules, important people, protocols, and so on. (Kevin also used that opportunity to tell them how smart they were—and that he knew it even though their grades didn't reflect their aptitude).

The point in describing this incident is that modern-day students are just as intelligent and capable of learning as they were a hundred years ago, but the constant changes in our culture demand that educators be cognizant of the current values and beliefs of students in their classrooms in order to be effective. It is our job to determine how to instill the value of education in our students and parents while respecting where they are coming from and to think about the activities that catch their attention and relate to *their* lives!

Educators can be angry all day long about the existence of gangs, but that isn't going to make them go away. We have to determine what our students value and then *use what they value* to teach them what we want them to know. We can start with our own values as an end in mind, but we have to start teaching by understanding what our students value first. Intuitively we know this, but our pride sometimes won't allow us to accept our students for who they are because we don't share the same values. We incorrectly believe that if we accept them for who they are *before* we start teaching them, then we're compromising our own beliefs. *We* are the cure for apathy, but we have to care enough to see that. If we don't have the cure, students will continue to *appear* to be apathetic about learning and continue to *be* apathetic about school. This concept isn't rocket science, but we haven't applied it to both our classrooms and our professional development activities.

Let's think about instruction in terms of what we do know in order to determine how we can develop effective instruction.

Instruction: Begin with the End in Mind

You've read a nonexample of twenty-first-century learning, so now let's focus on some good examples. Think about walking into the "perfect" classroom defined by adults who, at best, are trying to determine what students need to learn now—knowing it's hard to predict a kindergartner's world of work. What does it look like? Is the teacher standing up lecturing and are all of the students dutifully taking notes in a quiet fashion? Is the teacher asking questions and is every student in the room raising a hand without "oohing"? Are all the students wearing clothes that fit, that don't hang off their rear ends? Is Opie there? How about Beaver? If you're having problems picturing a classroom different than the one described, then the rest of this section will be beneficial for you.

Let's forget about Laura Ingalls Wilder, Beaver, and even Mr. Kotter's classroom for a while and revert to the purpose of classrooms and instruction. What is the purpose of a lesson or even a program of study? What are educators actually trying to accomplish? According to the Common Core State Standards Initiative (CCSSI) mission statement, "The standards are designed to be robust and relevant to the real world, reflecting the knowledge and skills that our young people need for success in college and careers. With American students fully prepared for the future, our communities will be best positioned to compete successfully in the global economy" (CCSSI, 2011). As of this writing, forty-seven states have adopted the CCSSI, so that mission statement should apply to the majority of the K–12 educators reading this text. If educators are supposed to be preparing students for the real world, then wouldn't it make sense to have our classrooms reflect the real world?

Considering traditional classrooms and how they operate, the classrooms in career or technical schools come closest to the twenty-first-century philosophy and the CCSSI mission statement, in the opinion of the authors (if you are familiar with career classes, think about how they differ from most core curriculum classes). Most career education courses are designed around problem-based learning. Wikipedia (2011) defines problem-based learning as "a student-centered pedagogy in which students learn about a subject in the context of complex, multifaceted, and realistic problems. . . . Working in groups, students identify what they already know, what they need to know, and how and where to access new information that may lead to resolution of the problem" (para. 1). Does this sound like twenty-first-century learning?

There are also reasons why these types of courses are appealing to students. First, students choose to take career education courses because they're interested in the occupation associated with the class or the development of a specific skill. In addition, they often get licensure for working in a specific area after graduating from a program of study at a career center school. What a concept! Students get to choose courses in which they're interested, and they understand the direct relationship between what they learn in those courses and their career choices. They're also using the same equipment in those courses that they will use in the real world.

Second, students rarely sit in straight rows of desks and listen to a lecture in career centers. Typically, they're up and working on a project that is appropriate to their skill level in the particular class. For example, seniors in welding classes are working on much more refined pieces of work than their sophomore or first-year counterparts, even though they are in the same class. The instructor differentiates their work based on their level of expertise, but they're all still learning about the concepts of welding. In addition, students are often working in groups on projects.

Finally, the instructor is working alongside students as they complete their projects. Typically, the instructor is up and moving around the classroom interacting with students, asking them questions about their work, and sometimes even helping them work out solutions to problems they have come across—and that the instructor may or may not have experienced before.

Are you asking yourself how you can make your classrooms look more like these career center classes, or are you explaining out loud to the authors why this cannot happen—or, perhaps, should not happen—in your school? If you're already thinking that lessons in your school cannot look like career center lessons, then you need to start thinking in smaller chunks—and about how to take the initial steps in addressing the professional development needs of your teachers.

Instructional Leadership in the Twenty-First Century

Tony Wagner, Douglas Reeves, and Malcolm Knowles are "heroes" for twenty-first-century learning. A combination of their philosophies asks instructional leaders to use adult learning theory to guide other educators through professional development activities that help them identify what they already know, what they need to know, and how and where to access new information leading to the resolution of complex, multifaceted, and realistic educational problems as a means to bring about an evolution in the K–12 instructional process that would ultimately prepare students for college or the workplace. That may sound complex, but try to think of making changes in small chunks. The following activity is just one example of how to initiate such a change.

One of the biggest mistakes principals make is pitting themselves against their entire staffs by taking a stand on a particular topic during a faculty meeting. Occasionally such a move is necessary, but usually it can and should be avoided. It makes more sense to have faculty members discuss topics among themselves to sort out problems or issues while the principal (or even lead teachers) facilitates the discussion. This way, the occasion doesn't become a "me vs. them" scenario.

Wrapping It Up

The *Using What You've Learned* activity at the end of this chapter will help you to build awareness about twenty-first-century learning and/or the CCSSI—and it is set up so that teachers do most of the work and develop their own conclusions about the topic (just as we want their students to do) as opposed to principals' declaring what they want teachers to do. Typically, teachers are overconfident about their grade-level standards, but they will usually admit that they have little knowledge of the vertical alignment of standards. One of the helpful traits of the CCSSI is that the standards neatly build off each other in a vertical fashion.

There is no question that twenty-first-century learning will change many times in your career and in the lives of the students you currently serve. But the important thing to consider about learning is whether you truly believe it is fluid and whether you are prepared to change as the need to change arises, for, truly, the only constant in the twenty-first century is change. Make it positive change for student learning.

USING WHAT YOU'VE LEARNED

Divide the teachers at your school into random vertical teams (this exercise also works well for principals in district meetings). Provide them with a list of grades, using all grades from K–12, no matter what level your school is. Take a sample of one strand of the CCSSI and remove the indicator that shows the grade level. Ask the teachers to discuss the standards one at a time and place them next to the appropriate grade level. Let the teams know that they will have one minute to discuss each standard, that each team needs to have a spokesperson to call out their answers, and that they will have an opportunity to change their answers as new standards are given to each table. These parameters will give the facilitator control of what the audience is going to *think* about!

Give the teams the following standard first: *Participate in collaborative conversations with diverse partners about [grade level] topics and texts with peers and adults in small and larger groups.*

Call on each team to give its answer and a quick reason why. Tally the responses where the entire group can see them. Then provide the correct answer, which is kindergarten. Specifically, the standard is kindergarten Speaking and Listening Standard #1 (SL.K.1).

At this point there is likely to be quite a bit of discussion in the room. The good news is that the teachers will be discussing their shock that this is a kindergarten standard (as opposed to a higher grade level) and not arguing with you about what you're trying to communicate. They're also probably gearing up for the next standard in order to get the answer correct—and with that expectation they have *already* recalibrated their expectations for grade-level standards! Once you've completed this activity, you've initiated a shift in the way your teachers think about the vertical alignment of standards.

You can actually take this exercise a step further by asking the teams to discuss how these standards might roll over into the fine arts, science, social students, and other non-ELA (English Language Arts) classes; have them report to the whole group what those lessons might look like. Again, you've put the duty on the teachers to communicate these ideas to other teachers—you're just facilitating the process.

After the initial standard, pick some standards that randomly fall within the grade levels at your school. For example, a middle-school principal might choose the following standard: *Delineate a speaker's argument and specific claims, evaluating the soundness of the reasoning and relevance and sufficiency of the evidence and identifying when irrelevant evidence is introduced.*

Wrap up by having each team choose one standard and identify what it will look like when students are engaged in learning that standard and what you, as principal, will be able to see as a result.

2

Building Trust

Expecting teachers to respect your position when you arrive at a school as its new principal is legitimately part of the fabric of socialization in our culture. But respecting the position and trusting the individual are not necessarily the same. Even if you are an experienced principal in a given school, you may need to step back and examine your relationship with the teachers. Do they have a basis for trusting you to lead them?

Trust: Given or Earned?

Jacque once taught a summer master's-level class on supervision of instruction that met all day Saturday with a break for lunch. Class members had read an article on building trust as a critical part of supervising adults in the school setting. Having told the students to think about trust over lunch, Jacque left to run an errand. On her way out the door of the college, an apparently homeless man asked her for food. She said, "I don't have anything, but I'm going to get lunch and I will bring you a sandwich. Just wait here." After finishing her errand, she bought some chicken sandwiches, including one for the homeless man. When she returned to the college, the man was gone.

As the class started, Jacque told the students about the man and the sandwich. She asked, "Why do you think he didn't wait?" One student said, "Oh, he really wanted you to give him money on the pretense of food and then he was going to buy booze or drugs." Another said, "Maybe it was because he had no basis for trust with you. You know that you are trustworthy, but his experience with other people 'like' you is that they do not come back with food. Isn't that really what you asked us to think about?"

The question applies to more than just chicken sandwiches. Why should others trust principals to lead them to better teaching? Can principals expect trust because of their positions or do they have to earn it?

While it is true that the role of the principal has moved from *principal teacher* in the early 1900s to *administrator* in the mid-twentieth century, it is clear that the role of the principal is different from the role of management in business and industry. As has often been said, "We do not build widgets; we educate people." Educating people is a part of the principal's job. But somewhere along the way educators seem to have lost the *teaching* aspect of the role of principal. The role of principal as leader of learning, for the benefit of students, is the heart of this book. Where can you have the most impact, whether you are a principal in preparation or a principal of long standing? Because every journey has to start somewhere, the authors suggest that sharing data provides the greatest likelihood of teaching, leading, and building trust.

Sharing Data with Teachers: Knowledge Is Power

Data flow around us continuously in life and in our work as principals—data regarding test scores, benchmarks, grades, attendance (of teachers and students), budgets, utilities, supplies, discipline referrals, books, socioeconomic level of students, gender and race of teachers and students, athletic and activity schedules, and on and on. Perhaps the subtitle of this section scares you a bit: *knowledge is power*. Did you read that and think that giving teachers data will give *them* power over *you* as the principal? Or did you think that giving teachers data will expand the power of all the educators in your building to work together to make a positive difference for the students you serve? The authors assume the latter.

In order to build trust, you need to distinguish between public and private when considering which data to share with teachers. For example, you need to examine which data are truly confidential and thus should be limited to need-to-know sharing. Teachers' personnel files are generally private (depending on the state). In some states, principals' evaluations of teachers are public except for the current year. Salaries are public information; in fact, the entire budget of a public school district is available to the public under the Freedom of Information Act. Yet many principals act as if the budget is their private domain. In most states, the principal is legally responsible to account for and manage the budget. But since budgets should be used to advance the mission of student learning, they should be considered in any list that you generate of data that you can or should share. The following example about sharing budget data is but one of many that can illustrate how building trust and using the power of educators to problem-solve can benefit the students that they serve.

Budget Information: To Share or Not to Share

In the first school where Jacque was principal, the copying costs were eating up the budget. The district had the tracking devices that allowed her to know who copied how much, but that made the job of principal one of policing. So her first sharing of budget information with teachers (who had never known the school budget) was to show them how much money was in the general revenue budget, the categories in which it was spent, and how much was spent in each category.

First, she asked the lead teachers to meet with their teams to consider why they needed copies and what other items they could buy that would be more important to them than copies. They generated a list; a few weeks later, the faculty met to discuss which grade levels and disciplines most needed copies and why. Then the lead teachers were asked to work together to propose a copy budget for each grade level and discipline.

The result? Teachers accepted responsibility for managing the copy budget. They understood how to allocate copying and knew that they could bring a request back to the lead teacher team if the system was not working as anticipated. They took the copy codes off the machine and Jacque later learned from the representative of the contracted copy company that their school had the lowest copy per teacher rate in the district. (He said, "Boy, you must really rule with an iron hand.")

Did she?

Building a List of Data as a Way to Build Trust

Close your door—yes, you really can do that! Generate a list of all the data available to you. If you need a place to start, look at the list at the beginning of the previous section or look at the types of data addressed in Chapter 4. Set your list aside for a day or two and come back to it. Ask your support staff (e.g., bookkeeper, secretary) and other administrators (e.g., assistant principals) to generate a list of data that they know is part of running the school. Compare their lists to yours. Add to your list any data they thought of that you didn't already have. Now you have a picture of all the data that you manage every day. Then share the list with teachers—either with all the teachers or a subset (e.g., team leaders, grade-level chairs, department heads). Ask them to examine the types of data that you have listed for your school and add any that you have overlooked. Now you have a list!

At this point, ask the teachers to think about the data that would be most important for them to know and understand in order to best serve student learning. Encourage them to talk to each other. Bring them back together either in small groups (e.g., departments, grade levels) or as a faculty and use the nominal group technique (described below) to determine the most important data sets to start the sharing of data.

How to Use the Nominal Technique

The easiest method is to take the number of data sets (N) and divide by 4 (i.e., N/4 = X). For example, if you have 12 sets of data on your list, divide 12 by 4 and you get 3. Then have each person in your group select the top three sets of data that they need to know and understand. This does not mean that the other data sets are not important; it is just that you have to start with something. At this point you can either have each person submit a top-three list and have someone record them, OR, if you have a safe, trusting environment, you can write the entire list on chart paper and have each person indicate his or her top three choices with a check or tally mark or three colored dots (available at office supply stores). (Although 4 is an arbitrary number by which to divide, it generally works well in arriving at a workable number of ideas.)

Once you have the list organized by priority based on the faculty's data set choices, you will need to develop a plan for how you will share and use the data. These first steps are described here because they are critical to developing trust with teachers so they know you are willing and able to share decision making with them. Chapter 4 will go into more detail on types of data that you can and should use in leading positive change for student learning and will help you examine data that you may need to develop. All data should be focused on enhancing student learning and creating a positive learning environment for each student.

Consider the following steps, adapted from a list provided by Pat Mayfield (2010) on building trust in the workplace. How would you rate yourself on these steps?

1. **Be honest:** The first step in building trust is to be honest.
    - Tell the truth. Even small lies and twisted truths are still lies.
    - Share honest information, even if it's to your disadvantage.
    - Don't steal—on expense reports from the supply cabinet or ideas from your colleagues.

2. **Use good judgment:** The second step is to know what information to share, when to share it, and when not to share it.
   - Protect employees' personal information and the school's proprietary information as if it were your own.
   - Think twice before sharing a blunt, unsolicited judgment. Extreme honesty may hurt the recipient, ironically destroying trust and the safe environment.
   - Don't expect apologies to erase your wrongdoings. Apologies might earn a forgive, but perhaps not a forget.
   - Avoid "just between us" secret conversations unless necessary for the benefit of the school.

3. **Be consistent:** The third step is to be consistent in words and behaviors. It's not enough to be trustworthy only on Tuesdays and Thursdays.
   - Show up—every day and on time—and stay at least the required hours.
   - Do the work; meet or exceed the job description and school standards.
   - Do what you say you will do. Fulfill your promises.

4. **Be honest in nonverbal communications:** Body language experts tell us that more than 50 percent of a statement's impact is nonverbal communication. To increase trust through body language:
   - Look others in the eye with comfortable and direct eye contact.
   - Exhibit open body language, including (1) open arms versus closed across the chest or hands clasped together, (2) hands kept in sight (not behind you or in your pockets) and open (not in a fist), and (3) legs uncrossed with feet flat on the floor, while seated.

5. **Have a mutually beneficial attitude:** Blatant self-serving agendas may cast doubt on one's trustworthiness. In reality, everyone has self-serving agendas, but it is the level of harm to others that determines the level of trust in that person. To increase trust:
   - Avoid me, me, me. Genuinely care about others and promote we, we, we.

- Nurture mutually beneficial relationships with open communications.
- Willingly accept information and constructive critique.

6. **Be a trustworthy leader:** Trusted leaders are sorely needed. Leaders should be able to:
    - Ask the hard questions to build and protect the school.
    - Listen and consider others' ideas with an open mind.
    - Focus on issues and solutions rather than personalities.
    - Set an example by being responsible and accountable.

Encouraging Teachers to Talk to and Share with the Principal

In 1992, when Jacque was a principal, the teachers' need to talk *with* her became most apparent when they acquired networked computers. Having been a college professor in special education prior to her decision to return to K–12 and become a principal (so that she could "save kids before they drowned"), Jacque knew well the belief system in higher education that faculty are colleagues. That is not a term that has been well accepted in the hierarchical structure of K–12 education. Glickman, Gordon, and Ross-Gordon (2004) offer clear definitions of three types of schools, with the most productive having a collegial nature. Yet rarely do K–12 faculty members or administrators refer to each other as colleagues. However, because of her strong belief that she and her teachers *must* be colleagues to truly address the needs of the students, she set out to develop and nurture an open, collegial environment. In the seven years of her principalship in one school, Jacque learned that it *is* possible to have a collegial environment based on mutual trust; a principal who is well-informed about the needs, goals, and aspirations of teachers; and a shared decision-making process based on that information and a commonly shared belief system. What she had not figured out was how to make the time to engage teachers individually and collectively in purposeful dialogue about their work. The running joke was, "We need to get the meat market ticket numbers so we know who gets to talk to the principal next." Once they had e-mail, Jacque realized that teachers wanted to discuss many things with her that they never had time to discuss. But e-mail helped. Management by e-mail is not sufficient for the academic development and smooth operation of a school, but it is a helpful tool allowing communication that is outside the day-to-day flow of things.

Although the volume of e-mail in today's world can be overwhelming, there are ways to use the tool to our advantage. The use of e-mail can lead to talking with teachers, which is an important benefit.

Replacing Outmoded Faculty Meeting Announcements

The need for dialogue on educational issues should be apparent to all educators. However, the time necessary to engage in such important discussions can be elusive, as noted by Hebert (1999):

> I confess! For more than 15 years I have not looked forward to faculty meetings. Over all this time, I've allowed our meetings to fall into the stereotypic pattern of dreaded mandated gatherings that jolt us from our teaching day into a 50-minute rapid firing of disconnected announcements and abbreviated discussions about issues that require much more time and thought. (p. 219)

In today's world of technology, faculty meetings should be reserved for discussion about educational issues; that "rapid firing of disconnected announcements" should be relegated to written newsletters, e-mail, and e-mail calendars. Most schools have e-mail; those who do not certainly have the ability to create a paper announcement system using a weekly newsletter (see Figure 2.1, page 26). Over the years, principals have said, "But if you put announcements in the faculty mailboxes, teachers won't read them." The logical response is "What makes you think they listen to verbal announcements?" To argue that schools should maintain an outmoded, nonproductive system of faculty meetings because one faculty member won't read the written word is like saying we should have continued using typewriters because not everyone could afford a computer (which was true, of course, but those same people probably didn't have a typewriter either!). If teachers don't read the faculty newsletter and the operation of the school is not affected, then maybe those announcements never needed to be said anyway. If an individual faculty member doesn't read the newsletter and therefore fails to meet a deadline, it is the perfect teachable moment for the principal to discuss with that faculty member why individual responsibility and participation are critical to the smooth operation and well-being of the entire school.

Another technique for sharing information is to send e-mails with informative, relevant subject lines (see Figure 2.2, page 28).

Figure 2.1 Sample Newsletter

Any School, USA
Weekly Newsletter
September 1, 2011

Action Needed

Put any information here (bulleted or numbered) that requires action on the part of all teachers and/or staff. For example, the following format can be helpful:

- Due September 13: All class lists must be checked, signed, and returned for funding verification.

Need to Know

Put any information here that does not require action but for which employees are held accountable. For example, the following format can be helpful:

- Technology equipment promised from the District Office has been delayed; we will be notified of anticipated arrival.

Other Matters

Put any information here that does not require action and that employees are not held accountable for knowing, but is of interest to them. For example, the following format can be helpful:

- There will be an inspector on campus related to new construction on Friday, September 10.

Celebrations and Thanks!

Put any information here that you (or others) want to share with everyone on the faculty and staff. For example, the following format can be helpful:

- The Math Wizards Club came in first in the district at the competition on October 9.
- Ms. Mary Smith has been appointed to the District Curriculum Committee for ELA.

Traveling this Week!

Put any information that you (or others) want to share with everyone on the faculty and staff. For example, the following format can be helpful:

- Mr. Jones and Mr. Coulter will be attending the MMGW regional meeting on Tuesday.

Date Reminder

This should be a running calendar of events that involve the school faculty and staff from the current week to the end of the year. Each time you send a newsletter, past events should be removed and new ones added in correct date order. For example, the following format can be helpful:

September 4, 7:00 p.m.—Open House—All faculty
September 6, 4:30 p.m.—Walk to School Day
September 20—report cards go home
December 21—last day before winter break
May 5—last day for students
May 9—last day for teachers

A third tool for sharing information is the calendar feature in the school's e-mail system. Many principals think they should devise a common calendar for the events that involve a large group or require the use of space, but although they might announce such events in a faculty meeting, there is rarely a centralized place to post a reminder so individuals don't have to enter it into their own calendar systems.

Dr. Sharon Buddin, former principal of Blythewood High School in South Carolina and NASSP National Secondary Principal of the Year in 2003, set up her own e-mail using three major components:

1. She labeled e-mail folders with helpful headings (e.g., Grade 9, Grade 10, Grade 11, Grade 12, URGENT, ACTION in 2 days, Budget, Read at leisure, PRIVATE, Secretary action, Discussion items)
2. She told faculty members to put PRIVATE in the subject lines of their e-mails to her if the secretary was NOT to read them.
3. She trained her secretary to open her e-mail, sort it, and file it in an appropriate folder.

This system allowed Buddin to read those e-mails that required immediate attention on her part, file them by grade level, return them to her secretary for action (if an e-mail required a letter to be sent, for example), and generally avoid spending all her time reading e-mail and acting on things that could be delegated. In earlier times principals relied on their secretaries to read their letters and organize them before giving them to the principal. Somehow principals lost that system when they started using electronic mail. Many administrators say they are bogged down with e-mail and don't have time to do the

Figure 2.2 Sample E-mail

> To: All faculty
>
> From: John Smith, Principal
>
> Subject: 4/8 due date for textbook orders to dept. leaders &
> 4/15 to office manager
>
> Textbook orders for next year are due to your department leaders no later than 4/8 so they can forward the orders to the office manager by 4/15. Please be sure you meet with your department leader in time to facilitate the timely submission of those orders. As always, thank you for your thoughtful decision making in regard to the educational materials available for our students.
>
> Respectfully, John

rest of their job. But using these technological tools will allow principals, faculty, and staff to share timely, updated information efficiently and reserve faculty meetings for their original purpose: discussing important educational issues.

Managing Discussions at Faculty Meetings

Once you are ready to use your faculty meeting time for discussions, you will want to consider how people deal with information.

One of the greatest perceived deterrents to dialogue among faculty and administrators is the "lack of time." Maybe the real issue is that they don't manage time well. They do not always use the tools and human resources available and sometimes administrators do not trust teachers and staff to always do what the administrator thinks is right. To engage others in dialogue on challenging issues requires (1) a willingness to explore ideas in a structured fashion, (2) preparation to conduct a session with agendas, and a structure that is open to extending the discussion if the need arises, and (3) commitment to clarifying the issue, identifying possible solutions, and following up with strategies to see the solution to completion (even when it doesn't work.) Jacqueline Jacobs's work on *Leading Learning in a Changing World: Using Children's Literature for Professional Dialogue* (Jacobs and Rotholz, 2005) evolved from her belief that children's literature is a strong metaphor for most issues in adult lives and a neutral framework for discussing difficult issues. But the primary goal is not the discussion, although that is critical and much needed;

it is the "insight into action" (Jacobs and Rotholz, 2005) resulting from the dialogue that is the key to productive solutions.

A major element in generating a discussion is to determine the mindset of the faculty and/or staff on an issue *before* you begin the discussion. It is not necessary to know specifically what each individual thinks. But it is crucial for all individuals to examine what they think before a discussion begins. Asking a couple of key questions, which do not have to be answered publicly, will allow the discussion participants to consider their own personal beliefs. This is an example of creating a teachable moment for teachers. If someone stands in front of the room and lectures on any given topic, the audience's ability and interest in attending to that information is contingent on many things (e.g., energy level, other tasks waiting to be done); however, if participants are invited to think about a topic before the discussion begins, they will be much more likely to think through the relevant issues and information and make meaningful contributions to the subsequent discussions.

For example, to start a faculty meeting discussion of the challenge of meeting the needs of students with Asperger's syndrome, the principal could ask the following:

1. Write an account of a bright student who takes things literally, particularly social cues.
2. Do you think all students are able to learn the value of social customs and mores? (Jacobs and Rotholz, 2005, p. 102)

So how do such questions and prompts lead to greater dialogue on the challenging issues that face teachers and administrators? Teachers generally participate in discussions when they are provided a neutral context from which to consider the topic. They are more willing to problem-solve when it is clear that the discussion has purpose and leads to action. The principal who is a leader of learning wants the opportunity to engage teachers in dialogue to a productive end, which of course may lead to many new beginnings.

Actions Arising from Dialogue

Even the most innocuous-seeming conversation with a teacher may require some sort of subsequent action on the part of the school administrator. The teacher's comment "You know, it would be nice if the soft drink machine in the faculty room could be moved to a corner—it creates so much heat that it is uncomfortable to sit near it" may have been said in passing, but the intent was to signal to the administrator that (1) here is an irritant that may actually result in bigger problems if not addressed, and (2) this issue is at least one that this individual is willing to bring to the principal's attention. If, after thorough investigation, you decide that the desired action is not possible at the time, you should give the faculty member the professional courtesy of explaining why the change cannot occur. Also, since your first action regarding an idea may not be the best, you should either (1) think about it overnight, (2) have it discussed in a wider forum, or (3) do both! Certainly, if you do nothing, you will have closed a door that may be much more difficult to open later.

Some school administrators have not learned that they are not the only person who can make a given action occur. In fact, the best leaders learn to delegate in very positive and creative ways. In the authors' experience, women administrators are much more likely to take on additional tasks because they think that is their job. Women in our society are socialized to be nurturers (aside from any biological predisposition) and that often carries over into the workplace. Of course, many men are also nurturers, but since the overwhelming majority of teachers are women, the tendency in women is possibly more apparent in education or just more accepted or expected. In a collegial environment, all individuals should be expected to help carry the load. This does not mean that school administrators abdicate their responsibility to lead. Quite the contrary, learning to delegate defines their leadership as respectful of the skills and rights of others and supportive of individual talent and ability to accomplish or facilitate tasks.

The result of every faculty meeting should be a specific plan for how a discussion will lead to action and what the evidence of that action will be. This agenda should include the due date for the action, when appropriate; the names of the people who are responsible for the action and for reporting back to the group; and the due date for that report. (See Figure 2.3.)

In modeling good teaching through the use of dialogue, principals are teachers of teachers and generate a far higher probability that teachers will consider their own teaching as they observe better models for ways to engage in learning.

Talking to Teachers

Clearly one of a principal's major responsibilities is to evaluate teachers and be an active participant in their development. Although the authors acknowledge that some principals find the conflict between development

Figure 2.3 Sample Faculty Meeting Agenda

Agenda Item	Person Leading	Materials Needed and/or "To Do" Prior to Meeting	Follow-Up and Person Responsible for Ensuring Completion	Due Date
Welcome	Ms. Jones, Assistant Principal	Teachers with student teaching interns should be prepared to introduce the interns		
Discussion: Supervision of students in halls	Mr. Smith, Lead Teacher	Review school policy. Think of possible solutions. Talk to students about possible solutions. Bring an open mind to the meeting.	Proposed plan	
Celebrations	Dr. Brown, Principal			

Information Item	Contact Person	Information Needed	Follow-Up Needed	Due Date
Third nine-week grades	Department heads/AP	Comments required on each student's report	Completed	3/29
Book orders	Department heads Office manager	Consult with DH on your needs.	Faculty submit to DH DH submit to OM	4/8 4/15
Professional learning day	Grade-level APs	9–12 workshop 2:30–3:30 teamwork on strategies from workshop	Implementation of new strategies will be focus of classroom visits starting on due date	Workshop: 4/10 Visits: starting 4/17

and the processes of summative evaluations a major challenge, the purpose of this section is to help principals think about the ways that they can construct meaningful interactions that will allow teachers to view themselves as lifelong learners. The most important key is the concept of evidence.

In the authors' work with students in a graduate course they co-taught on supervision of instruction, they used a systematic process for developing and practicing their skills in observation and feedback. As an individual principal, you may have to think through these strategies and practice them on your own. In an ideal world, you might ask another administrator to participate with you in developing the skills of gathering evidence and making evidence-based decisions.

The first step in creating a mind-set of operating from evidence is to gather information, or data, which can be either formal or informal. For example, one strategy is to randomly stop students and say, "Hi! I hope you had a great day today. Tell me one thing you learned." Do not *ask* the student what she learned; use the statement "Tell me . . ." Even the students who are perceived to have the most recalcitrant behaviors will generally tell you *something*! When you are in classrooms (you *are* in classrooms, aren't you?) every day, make sure you are observing students as well as teachers and making notes of specific evidence of engagement on the part of both. It is sad that in the last eight or ten years the authors have taught literally hundreds of graduate students who said they had not been visited by a principal in weeks, months, and, yes, even years. Don't allow yourself to say you do not have time to visit classrooms because you do *not* have time *not* to be in classrooms.

Using Positive, Objective, Prescriptive Language

In order to help teachers develop objective views of themselves as teachers, there has to be conversation about teaching. How you talk to teachers is important! By focusing on evidence rather than opinion, you can provide positive, objective feedback that can lead to improved learning environments for students. *Positive*, in this context, doesn't necessarily mean "pleasurable"; it means that your feedback is adding to the teachers' knowledge of their own teaching. *Objective* means that your feedback is based on observed evidence, not hearsay or opinion. *Prescriptive* refers to your agreed-upon plan based on your discussion of the classroom learning environment (see Figure 2.4). Few of us see ourselves as teachers the way our students do or as others do. There is more and more evidence that if we are to respond to the demands for student performance, we have to focus our observations of teaching on learning, rather than on teachers' "performing."

Figure 2.4 Observing for Evidence of a Positive Learning Environment

According to Stronge (2002), the teacher should demonstrate these positive qualities:

- ❑ Assumes ownership for the classroom and the students' success
- ❑ Uses personal experiences as examples in teaching
- ❑ Understands feelings of students
- ❑ Communicates clearly
- ❑ Admits to mistakes and corrects them immediately
- ❑ Thinks about and reflects on practice
- ❑ Displays a sense of humor
- ❑ Dresses appropriately for the position
- ❑ Maintains confidential trust and respect
- ❑ Is structured, yet flexible and spontaneous
- ❑ Is responsive to situations and students' needs
- ❑ Enjoys teaching and expects students to enjoy learning
- ❑ Looks for the win-win solution in conflict situations
- ❑ Listens attentively to students' questions and comments
- ❑ Responds to students with respect, even in difficult situations
- ❑ Communicates high expectations consistently
- ❑ Conducts on-on-one conversations with students
- ❑ Treats students equally and fairly
- ❑ Has positive dialogue and interactions with students outside the classroom
- ❑ Invests time with single students or small groups of students outside the classroom
- ❑ Addresses students by name
- ❑ Speaks in an appropriate tone and volume
- ❑ Works actively with students

Wrapping It Up

While considering the ways in which a leader builds trust, the most important thing to remember is that trust is earned: by the principal and by teachers. Your efforts to share information with teachers, whether budget data or test scores, will send clear messages that you are a team. Creating and developing an atmosphere of shared trust and respect among teachers and the principal will lead to trust among teachers and students—a win for all!

USING WHAT YOU'VE LEARNED

Using a quick paper survey or an electronic tool like SurveyMonkey (2010), ask teachers and staff to respond to these three questions. If using a paper survey, have them return the surveys to your secretary.

1. Give one example of action on the part of the principal that demonstrates that he or she trusts you to make good professional decisions.
2. Give one example of something the principal could or should do to demonstrate trust in teachers and staff.
3. Complete this sentence: My trust level in the principal as a leader of learning in our school is ________________ (very high, high, low, very low). In twenty-five words or less, tell why you made your choice.

Once you have this information, read it carefully and decide on two or three things you can do to improve trust in your leadership.

3

Change

"The illiterate of the 21st century will not be those who cannot read and write, but those who cannot learn, unlearn, and relearn" (Toffler, 1998). Change is infinite. The cars, phones, computers, and televisions that we use have changed drastically in just the last ten years. Who would have thought in the year 2000 that by 2009 a person could make a free video phone call to anyone in the world using the Internet, that thirteen-year-old children having cell phones would be the norm, and that VHS tapes would be almost obsolete? Online banking and online shopping have also changed the way in which consumers go about purchasing everything from coffee to houses. A person leaping in time from ten years ago would be shocked by all the changes in society—largely due to advances in technology. However, that same person would not notice much change in K–12 schools at all. For the most part, students still sit in rows of single-unit desks with textbooks in hand while a teacher lectures in front of the class. Why haven't our schools changed with the changing society around them? Some schools have "new" technology that teachers use as tools in the classroom (to replace the conventional dry erase board and, dare we say, overheads), but do classrooms function much differently than they did even fifty years ago?

"Who first used the term 'voodoo economics,' and what is another name for that concept?" the teacher asks the class while peering into the faces of her students to try to determine who knows the answer. Several students slump in their seats, fearing that they will have to reveal that they do not know the answer. Are they afraid of how the teacher will respond, or are they afraid of what the other students might think of them—or both?

At an early age, students quickly learn that not knowing the answers to the teacher's questions can mean big trouble. Students feel either guilt imposed by the teacher for not knowing answers or embarrassment imposed by bullying peers. In turn, students label themselves as inferior to classmates who *do* know the answers.

Perhaps, as educators, we are guilty of developing a culture in our own schools that cripples adults in the years to come. As students, we learned to hide any lack of knowledge for fear that others would look down on us or embarrass us. Now, as educators, we may still have others around us in supervisory positions who seem to wait for an opportunity to catch us not knowing the answer to something. Consequently, we are often hindered by our own fears of how others may perceive us.

Perhaps, as teachers, it would be more beneficial to ask questions nobody could answer, then allow students to do the needed research. Therefore, the ability to seek and find answers would be held above existing knowledge. This simple practice would reinforce to students (and ultimately to adults) that when it comes to information or knowledge, acquisition is far more important than recall. The future will require us all to be better at critical thinking skills than simple recall of trivial facts.

It is 2011. A high-school principal is holding an input meeting with various stakeholders, including one student, about the design of a twenty-first-century classroom. Teachers and administrators call out ideas about the placement of numerous outlets and data drops, LCD projectors, large-screen monitors, and various lighting styles. A teacher suggests that the school purchase a number of electronic picture frames to place along the wall to serve as small monitors so that students can view electronic portfolios as they are being developed. At each suggestion of an upgrade, the principal alludes to a tightening budget. They all digress to a discussion about how obsolete some of their current technology is that they spent so much money on just a few years ago—including laptops.

The tenth-grade student has been listening with interest to the conversation. At the mention of laptops, he blurts out, "You know, we could save money by just dismantling the old laptops and using their monitors instead of the electronic picture frames." The room goes silent—for several reasons. First, the adults do not know if what the student said is possible, so they do not know whether to agree with him or to dismiss his suggestion. Second, they are all in shock that one of their students has just suggested a way to save money that they have never thought of themselves. Finally, they all suddenly realize that they should have invited more students to participate in the discussion.

In today's world, the appropriate response to this suggestion would be to thank the student for such a creative idea, to ask him to investigate the possibilities of the idea, and, better yet, to offer him the chance to bring the idea to life in the form of a cross-content assignment, with classmates of his choice, for credit. In the best-case scenario, the student and some of his classmates could be given an assignment to work with a local architect to design their own twenty-first-century classroom. The problem is that far too many instructional leaders would never give the idea enough credit to investigate any further for fear that they would look stupid for asking about it.

In addition, most principals do not feel a sense of urgency regarding a need to change the way they think about school. Perhaps they do not see "school," or how we educate students, as an evolving process because it has been done the same way for so long. Like the legislators who create educational policies, principals and teachers were successful in the way they "did school" when they were younger, so why should they think they need to do anything different today?

Changing Culture

How does one go about changing the culture of the adult population in an educational setting in order to make individuals feel comfortable enough to admit that they need help—or comfortable enough to discuss the notion that maybe the way they are running the school is not the best way to do it? As with most types of change in the school setting, principals must take the first step in creating this change. Principals have to create *systems* by which educators acquire new knowledge and skills. Principals cannot take for granted that all teachers will have the self-motivation and initiative to learn on their own. However, the ultimate goal should be to have educators intrinsically motivated to seek needed knowledge and to try new ideas on their own, as well as to teach their students the skills they need to do the same.

The principal must take the lead initially by modeling behaviors conducive to the acquisition of knowledge in order to encourage teachers to engage in the same behaviors. The process begins with the principal standing in front of the faculty and simply stating, "I don't know everything about X and perhaps neither do you—and that's all right!" Perhaps it is easiest to explain this process through a concrete example. Let's go back to a time when new technology was introduced into the educational setting, so that we have a common perspective. For example, when interactive whiteboards were introduced, there was obviously a need for teachers to learn how to use them in the classroom effectively.

Far too many principals and school districts are focused on securing funds to acquire and install interactive whiteboards in their classrooms without making a conscious effort to create a vision for the technology's implementation. They never thought about how whiteboards could change the function of the classroom. Principals were not educated in their use; they merely knew that interactive whiteboards were a new technology that the faculty wanted, and there was a perception that they were needed. The tech-savvy and self-driven teachers learned how to exploit this new tool to its fullest advantage, but the principals failed to utilize these self-driven teachers, or "lead learners," to their fullest potential, neglecting to take advantage of their drive in order to inspire others. Meanwhile, the teachers who were less educated in the use of technology and the undermotivated underutilized the new machines.

When interactive whiteboards were first introduced, the principal should have taken the first step in modeling a desire to learn about them. She should have simply picked up the phone and called for help—from a colleague with more experience, a vendor that could provide training, or someone at the district office who could provide more information. If the principal was fortunate enough to have a "lead learner" on staff with experience in the use of interactive whiteboards, then she should have sought out his expertise. The principal could have encouraged him to take the leadership role in training the staff. During training, principals must be active learners and teachers need to witness that behavior in order for the training to carry any value.

Obviously, this process would have required the principal to admit that she lacked knowledge about the practical use of the interactive whiteboard in the classroom and that the expert teacher knew more. Some principals ask, "What is my faculty going to think of me when I tell them that I don't know something about classroom instruction?" The authors' flippant response to that question is, "What do you think they think of you when you pretend to know everything?" Far too many principals make the mistake of failing to admit that they do not know everything—or pretending that they know more than every one of their teachers. They believe that they are expected to be infallible experts in every complex skill, technology, or concept that is used in their building. Driving ahead on every educational initiative while faking expertise about it is as senseless as pretending to have knowledge about skydiving and then jumping out of a plane.

Principals not only have to unlearn the false expectation that they are supposed to know everything, but they also have to create an atmosphere of trust that allows everyone in the building to feel comfortable expressing a lack of knowledge about any topic. More importantly, principals have to give permission for everyone to make mistakes during the learning process—especially themselves. In this scenario, the principal should announce to the faculty that she has made inquiries about the product, that she needs to know more about it in order to make a sound decision about its use in the classroom, and that she values the opinion of the faculty before making a final decision.

Making It Work

The steps below could be used as an outline when introducing a new idea or concept to the faculty when the principal is not completely familiar with what is being introduced. Keep in mind while reading these steps that, at any given point, the principal could delegate these actions to someone else in the building while she takes on the role of facilitator—and active learner.

1. **Introduce the new idea.** Arrange for an expert to offer a demonstration of a new idea or concept. Notify faculty members ahead of time so that they can come prepared with questions and ideas in order to have input on whether the idea or concept should be implemented in the school. Allow them to ask as many questions of the expert as they like—and model questions yourself. Allow teachers to see that you still seek knowledge and that you do not have a predetermined notion about the use of the idea or concept.

2. **Discuss uses (how the idea will ultimately affect student achievement).** Lead the faculty and staff in a discussion about the use of the idea or concept and its potential impact on student achievement. They should understand that just because an idea or concept may be intriguing, a new fad, or recommended by your district does not necessarily mean that it will have a positive impact on student achievement in your school. Facilitate a productive conversation based on evidence (discussed in Chapter 4) about the proposed idea.

3. **Create a vision (what it would look like in the classroom).** Have teachers work in groups to paint a picture of what this product would like look if it were being used appropriately to impact student achievement in the classroom. Also ask them to describe what this would look like if it were used inappropriately in the classroom. Teachers have to be allowed to create their own vision for instructional practices in their classrooms in order to take ownership of them.

   Also ask teachers to list some ways that training with the product would work for your school. Some will prefer to learn in large groups, others in department- or grade-level teams and others individually. Guide them through making good decisions by providing limitations on the training process, such as funding and time restraints.

4. **Set goals (professional development, observations, resources, etc.).** Have teachers create measurable goals regarding the use of the product (how often it will be used per week or per day, for example) in small groups, and then discuss them in a large-group setting. This procedure gives everyone a common understanding of the expected use of the product in the school. Take the proposed goals suggested by the faculty and work them into a rubric for easy understanding. Reinforce the idea that although training will be provided for all teachers, they are ultimately responsible for their own learning. That expectation has to include their seeking help when they need it. In addition, make sure that you work with your leadership team to create measurable goals for yourself and each member of your team. Share them with the faculty, so they see that you're taking an active role in this process as well.

5. **Monitor goals.** Have the teachers share ideas about how the goals will be monitored. Will someone check their lesson plans for evidence? Will there be authentic student work or other artifacts that reflect the use of the product? Will the leadership team look for evidence during learning walks (or focus walks)? Will you provide an open line of communication for teachers to express their ideas and concerns about the strategy?

6. **Evaluate.** Evaluation is a key component of the implementation of any instructional strategy or program. Sometimes administrators add to teachers' workloads without taking anything away from them. Educators need to evaluate what is working for students in order to determine what to keep and what to throw away. To keep the process objective, appropriate evaluations of instructional programs should really be completed by an outside entity. However, not everyone has the financial resources available to pay outside evaluators or the appropriate support personnel in district offices. Instead, a simple first step in the evaluation process would be to discuss the goals you have established with your teachers and then discuss an appropriate tool to measure that goal. Is it going to be summative or formative assessment data, qualitative

data from students and teachers, or something else? Chapter 4 discusses some potential sources of data to help you and your faculty evaluate instructional programs and strategies.

7. **Adjust.** As you monitor and evaluate the implementation of any strategy or program, you and your teachers have to be willing to adjust. As stated at the start of this chapter, change is infinite. As the needs of your students change, the way in which you use various instructional strategies will need to change with them. Before initial implementation, it is important to communicate with the faculty that adjustments will be needed as you all learn about the best use of the strategy to meet the needs of your students.

Wrapping It Up

The authors have addressed some strategies for creating change on a small scale by outlining how to introduce new ideas to your faculty. However, creating infinite change by having adults rethink how schools operate is obviously a much larger task. Rhodes (2003) provides a scenario that makes creating major shifts in the way educators think about school almost impossible to realize:

> Seeking resources from the public for widespread changes in roles and relationships among adults is as counterintuitive as an airline's suggestion that you put on your oxygen mask before helping the child that accompanies you. Our culture's concern for children's well-being is so strong that it makes it almost impossible to have a more total perspective in which the relationship among all elements can be seen and their interdependence understood. (para. 23)

We create in our minds an infinite ethical battle when we make the education of our students a priority over our own education about how to best educate our students. It is difficult to justify the idea that we should stop the way in which we currently teach, which we inherently believe to be working based on our prior experiences, in order to learn something new. That would mean that we would have to use our current students as guinea pigs to try out a whole new way of thinking about school for the benefit of future students.

Creating a cultural shift in how educators think about schools, however, isn't going to be as drastic and as identifiable as showing up to work in a

Volkswagen van one day and in a hybrid sedan the next. Educators will not be forced to stop what they are doing and then start something new. This shift, rather, should look more like a scientific study of educational strategies by current practitioners who start to rethink what they are doing in schools.

As you continue to read this book, you will undoubtedly think about change in your own workplace. Being open to change yourself will enhance the probability that your faculty, staff, students, and parents will learn that change can be an opportunity, not a burden.

USING WHAT YOU'VE LEARNED

Identify a major change that occurred in your school—for example, in scheduling. Quickly write the answers to these questions:

1. How did you feel about the process surrounding the change?
2. Were you a leader in the change, an active follower, or a reluctant participant? How did your role affect how you felt about the process surrounding the change?
3. Identify, for yourself, two or three leaders, two or three active followers, and two or three reluctant participants for a change needed in your school (e.g., in discipline policy).
4. Put a note in your calendar to revisit these notes in ten days. At that time, schedule a meeting with the people you identified in Step 3 and use the section called *Making It Work* (page 39) to develop a plan to effect the change.

4

Assessing the Need for Change

Knowing Your School

Analyzing student achievement results does not change future student achievement results. What does? The authors may be stating the obvious here, but have you ever thought that the summative assessment information for your school, specifically from standardized tests, was a bit vague? It may provide very specific information about the percentage of students on grade level in your school and may even drill down to specific standards, but it doesn't tell you what happened in the classroom. In other words, it doesn't tell you what the teacher was doing right or wrong. It's a bit like seeing the final score of a sports event and having to draft a practice plan to address the needs of your players—when you didn't even watch the game! Yet, as educators, we spend a lot of time "looking at the data," usually meaning summative assessment data, to try to determine how to improve student achievement levels. An individual who supervises principals recently put this concept into a great phrase: "My principals do a wonderful job of looking at their test scores and admiring their problems."

Assessment Data

The big test! We are all very guilty of fearing "the test." That fear may be due to a focus on accountability testing through pieces of legislation like *No Child Left Behind* or our own insecurities about being judged. These often dreaded, often overhyped tests are summative in nature. They give us the big-picture information that allows us to examine the "whole" of our schools. But to shape instruction, yes, to lead learning, we have to focus on formative assessment. And regardless of the reason for the avoidance and fear, the lack of using assessments for instructional and monitoring purposes, as opposed to

Reflecting . . .

> When you finish reading the following statement, close your eyes and quickly think of your answer. Ready? Identify two or three sources of data that you deal with regularly. Do it!
>
> One of the most common things the authors have observed when talking with principals about data is that they immediately consider anything that has to do with numbers—test scores, number of discipline referrals, percentage of students getting free or reduced lunch. Why is that? The authors often ask teachers and principals why they track race, ethnicity, gender, attendance, and so on. They rarely know. Simple answer? Because they can! And, more importantly, why do educators use those same data to describe students and their test scores? Again, because they can!
>
> People and their relationships are complex: birth order, number of siblings, age of parents, socioeconomic status (other than measured by eligibility for free or reduced lunch), number of schools attended, and on, and on . . . Will educators consider these things? Should they? Data are as "simple" as numbers on some defined characteristic and as complex as the interactions of multiple data sources. How do they acquire and use multiple forms of data?

summative and evaluative purposes, is one of the major pieces of the educational puzzle that is missing in too many schools and classrooms. Formative assessments should be used for making 90 percent of the instructional decisions in a school. In short, they provide the information that should drive what the teacher is doing in the classroom as well as the direction of the school renewal or strategic plan.

Rather than focus on accountability testing, in order to lead learning it is important to understand the purpose of formative assessments. The easiest way to think about formative assessments is to think about them as "forming instruction." The results of these types of assessments provide teachers with information to shape their instruction. If a teacher has just covered adding double-digit numbers and gives a formative assessment to the class specific to that topic, then the results of that test will be used to determine which students and what percentage of students have mastered that skill, which ones need more help, and whether or not the class as a whole is ready to move on to the next topic. In addition, the results may be used to determine how the teacher might tailor homework assignments to meet the specific mastery level of the student. When using the results for homework, teachers should clearly understand the purposes of homework. Vatterott (2010) provides five hallmarks of good homework: purpose, efficiency, ownership, competence, and aesthetic appeal. Likewise, it is important that results from formative assessments are not used to provide grades for a student. The issues surrounding grading are so important that *Educational Leadership* dedicated a full issue (November 2011) to the topic of effective grading practices. Worth reading!

Throughout this chapter, the authors will talk about the kinds of data, formative and summative, that are available to instructional leaders. All data can be useful in terms of changing instructional strategies, but let's focus on annual summative information for now. Let's face it—test scores are the highlight of the school year and the information for which most principals and teachers are held accountable. In addition, there is certainly useful information in annual summative reports that instructional leaders must know in order to make informed instructional decisions. However, holding educators accountable for this information alone tends to make them focus on changing year-end results as opposed to focusing on the behaviors that influence those year-end results.

Kevin once heard football coach Lou Holtz discuss a missed opportunity for a touchdown in the final seconds of a game when a player dropped a pass in the end zone "that cost them the game," according to a reporter. The media tried to focus on the final play as the reason the team lost. Coach Holtz was quick to point out a lot of plays that went wrong during the entire game. His point was that one play doesn't determine the outcome of the game, and one player is not able to lose a game for the team; how every player plays during the entire game determines the outcome of the game. Undoubtedly, the entire coaching staff and every player spent many hours reviewing the video footage of that game in order to define exactly what worked and what didn't work, and the practices in the following week would have been designed to target those *specific* weaknesses; in addition, the staff likely designed plays to make the most efficient use of the team's best players. Why should strategic planning for a school be any different?

Like good football coaches, principals need to know the final score and the statistics of their players, but they also need to watch the entire game—and make decisions and changes as they progress through the school year. As educators, our typical attempt to achieve our goal is to buy programs and products in a constant search for that silver bullet that will bring up test scores. We go to conferences, we send our teachers to conferences, we ask other people what they're doing that works; we compare our demographics and other school characteristics to those of successful schools and make excuses about why their situation is different from our own. Or we buy a product that other schools are using and sit back and hope for the best. At the end of the year we wonder what went wrong. To put it simply, we're not watching the game. Even when we purchase products and implement them, we too often don't monitor the fidelity of their use. We need to get better at understanding what information is pertinent to improving instruction for the specific students we serve, understanding how to access that information in a usable format, and then using that information to improve what we are doing.

Knowing Your Students

You already know the many arguments that swirl around testing. Some students enter school already able to handle the second-, third-, or even fourth-grade curriculum. Others enter barely able to speak a three- or four-word sentence. A friend's now-grown son was speaking in eighteen-word sentences at two. When he turned five, his father said, "Kindergarten is the best place for him to learn socialization. We can teach him and keep him challenged intellectually." Jacque said to the child, "Darryl, your dad was just telling me that you are starting kindergarten. What do you think of that?" He responded, "It is okay, but I probably should be in grade three or four." Jacque said, "Really, why?" He said, "Because I already know half as much as I'm not supposed to know." So why is it that the data were clear on this child and he still had to start school in kindergarten? Socialization is undoubtedly a major function of kindergarten, but we have increasingly minimized that aspect of kindergarten, which might serve the Darryls of the world well, but may actually lead to the frustrations that many teachers and students experience as they move through school because the students never had time to learn to work in groups . . . you know, play nice with others! What data are you collecting and considering in order to know whether there really is reduced "playing nice with others" time?

Sharing . . .

Identify the elements of the conversation you will have with kindergarten teachers to look at how the new Common Core State Standard listed below relates to "playing nicely with others": *Prepare for and participate effectively in a range of conversations and collaboration with diverse partners, building on others' ideas and expressing their own clearly and persuasively* (CCSSI, 2011).

Suggestion: Have one group of teachers identify evidence for knowing that students "play nice with others." Give another group the new standard and ask them to identify evidence that students have met the standard. What are the differences? Similarities? Does the new standard change anything about the learning environment?

So what do *you* think? Is the new Common Core State Standard really another way of saying "learning to play nice with others" and therefore teachers can generate evidence of how language is used during play time?

In addition to the standards and typical testing data, which often differ from district to district, as well as state to state, an uncountable number of personal experiences influence and affect the students that you serve. Educators have to have the conversations about the students served in *each* school by the unique group of adults in their learning environments. We have to quit talking about what parents can or cannot do and what they do or do not do. Educators are the adults present for the six to eight hours a day students are in our schools (whether virtual or bricks and mortar). We have to learn about and figure out *how* to actively engage each student in each school, under the tutelage of those paid to teach them, in learning for their own growth and development.

At a recent state meeting of superintendents, a legislator spoke eloquently and passionately about charter schools legislation (Glazier, 2011), citing the origination of interest in charter schools as places to develop innovative learning environments that would speak to the needs of students not well served in traditional schools. Jacque sat listening to this speech, thinking, "Why do we have 'traditional' schools? What tradition? Schools were developed to serve a factory model of work. Why can't we see each school as a unique place of learning—a place where principals and teachers work together to create (remember Bloom's revised taxonomy?) active, engaged, twenty-first-century learners—a place where educators both invite and encourage parent involvement, but do not excuse lack of active learning by blaming parents who are not present during the time we are teaching their children?" One theme that continually emerges both in what the legislator said and in schools around the country is "We don't have time." But as a smart middle-school principal recently asked, "What student has a minute to waste while we figure it out?"

Data Sources

Use the collected data you have on students and use it wisely. Match the data sets so that you are looking at all aspects of a student on which you have data. In the following example, the grade level really doesn't matter because the strategy can be used at any level. It is, however, a true story. A principal and an assistant principal in an intermediate school (grades 5–8) set up an Excel spreadsheet to track discipline referral data for their students, including the defined data in the system (race, gender, socioeconomic status), coded teacher data (assigning a number to each teacher), coding for place of offense (class, halls, outside building, etc.), and type of offense (using the district coding system). (Some district systems for tracking discipline have all this data, and principals can easily extract it for analysis.) They then sorted the data by student and found that 90 percent of the discipline referrals in the school involved eighteen students; the offenses occurred overwhelmingly outside of classrooms in less structured and more social environments. So the administrators' solution was to divide the eighteen students between them and then make it their business, for two weeks, no matter what, for each to see those nine students every day *before* school started. This way they could gauge the emotional readiness of each student to begin the school day. There was some pushback from teachers because a student was late to first period or because the administrators were devoting time to "these" students, but the connections they built with the eighteen repeat offenders made a difference. Within a month, seventeen of the eighteen students were down to no referrals or no more than two a month. The eighteenth student had multiple issues, but the principal was able to engage other services and map a long-term plan for the student.

The students learned that they could seek assistance *before* they got into trouble—a win-win for the individual students, a productive use of the time that the administrators were spending with these students versus a punitive action in time that would have been spent dealing with a discipline referral. They used data, some of which they had to build into their spreadsheet since their district system didn't collect the data (place of offense), to help solve the problem and build solutions.

Using and Collecting Data

Sometimes the information educators need to meet the needs of students is not available in current data collection systems. You should collect or create new data only if it is going to be used in productive ways to improve learning for students. And a student's right to privacy must always be paramount in your decision as to what you collect and why.

Another aspect of using student data, which is not student specific, is gathering input on what educators do from students. K–12 educators have not generally followed a model of gaining students' input on any aspect of their day: not on teachers, not on their learning environment, not on discipline policies. Some schools do use student councils to provide input on student activities, such as planning the high-school prom, holding fund-raisers for a worthy cause, and occasionally even helping to solve problems like trash on a school campus. But there are many other things we could learn from student input.

Reflecting . . .

> For which of the following could you gather input from students through a survey or focus group?
>
> 1. Managing tardies in a middle school or high school
> 2. Considering the length of a class period (block) in a middle school or high school
> 3. Things that students like or dislike about their day in a given class or the whole school

Some of you will think, "We do a student survey at the end of the year." That's great! What do you do with the data? Principals often talk about the challenges of students' or teachers' behavior, but rarely conclude, "Based on our end-of-year survey information from students, we have realized that we need active student participation on our Leadership Team, not just token student representation. So we are working with our student council to establish an ongoing process for student engagement in the governance of our school." One high-school student commented about what he saw as a crackdown involving the policy that required teachers to lock doors at the tardy bell: "I often wonder why teachers and principals set rules without talking to us. I know people who walk just slowly enough to be sure the door will lock in a class they don't want to go to anyway. Some days they get caught and have detention, some they don't, because the teacher often doesn't mark us tardy. If they'd just ask us why we don't want to go to class, or figure out why there are some teachers that all kids want to be in their class, they might not need a rule for being tardy." If only educators paid more attention to the wisdom of the young!

If we, as educators, care about improving schools, we need to rethink the data we *want* in order to ensure that we improve *learning* environments, not just *teaching* environments. Following are some examples of data you can generate from students.

♦ Survey students and/or parents who are leaving your school. Here are three simple questions that could be part of a checkout procedure, either asked by someone in the office or developed in a tool like SurveyMonkey:

  - What was the best part of being a student at this school?
  - Identify one thing that would have made this school better for you (your child).

- Identify one thing you wish you (your child) had been able to study at this school that you (your child) did not get to study.

♦ Survey students and/or parents who are new to your school. Here are three simple questions you can ask:

  - Tell us one thing that you think makes a school a great place for you (your child) to be.
  - If you (your child) could study anything in this school that you wanted to study, what would it be?
  - What do we need to know to help you (your child) be an active learner in this school?

♦ Conduct focus groups with students who teachers think will be both supporters and naysayers on a topic in order to collect student perspectives. Focus groups should be led by someone trained and/or experienced in leading groups, including establishing norms so the group members know how to participate.

Whether you use surveys, focus groups, or just conversations with students, remember that the purpose of gaining information is to help you improve the learning environments in your school. The idea is for you to consider the importance of knowing and caring what your students think and believe about their learning and the environment to which they come each day. The information can refer to the structure of the school, the curriculum, the instruction, the facilities, and so on. One student who had just finished eighth grade was asked to identify the best teacher he ever had. Without hesitation he named "Mrs. D, my social studies teacher," because "at the beginning of the year, she showed us all the standards we had to meet that year. She said, 'I have all these materials available, we have a library, we have a computer lab and two computers in our room. I am a resource. So how will you accomplish all these standards and how will I know that you know it?' and then she put us in groups and had us make a plan for how we could learn the standards for the first nine weeks." Imagine! Mrs. D trusted *them*, the students, to think about and help develop the ways they would learn and apply their knowledge. A number of parents whose children had her as a teacher also label her the best teacher their children ever had. Why?

Probably no one has asked Mrs. D. about her views on teaching and learning outside of her personal conversations with whatever colleagues she has chosen to discuss her work. But, as suggested earlier, there are too few schools where the conversations among teachers and administrators occur in a defined way to examine teaching and learning. All schools need to have teams of teachers working together just as teachers should have students working together. Principals need to know what teachers know and believe.

Knowing Your Teachers

In public schools today, administrators are often unsure of the teachers' roles. Teachers are employees, but many teachers act as autonomous contractors; they are professionals, but in many schools they are treated like hourly workers; they are educated, but in many schools their views are not sought or valued. What do you know about your teachers? What do you believe about their roles?

There was a time when the teacher *was* the school. Small towns had one-room schools with no administrators, no bureaucracy to speak of, just a place where an adult worked with children and young people in the teaching and learning process. Over the twentieth century, all but a few of those schools evolved into centralized places of learning as motorized buses arrived in the 1930s and as efficiencies came into play. An even more dramatic change occurred during desegregation when buses became the mechanism for ensuring integrated school settings. As the management of schools became more centralized and administrators evolved from principal teachers, the early principals in our country, more and more controls were placed on teachers. It seems a long time since there was any public conversation or debate about who teachers are. Do you know what the teachers in your school know and believe about teaching and learning? Do you know what ideas they have about improving the learning environment for students?

Although teachers are paid to teach, much of the rhetoric heard today suggests that many teachers consider themselves independent contractors in a system that considers them employees. They work in a community that wonders what it would be like to work "nine months a year" (those same people rarely think about what it is like to be responsible for 20 to 120 students each day and that teachers only get paid to work those nine months with no mechanism for earning more) and in a society where we are all concerned to educate children and young people so they can eventually earn a living and perpetuate the society's values and standard of living.

Just as there are any number of ways you can determine your school's progress toward a given behavior or goal, there are any number of ways you can collect data to determine what your teachers know, believe, and act upon. The simplest way, of course, is to just ask. You could establish a focus group

Reflecting . . .

> A new principal was particularly focused on shared decision making. She believed that if a group of professionals could truly work together to create or enhance the learning environment for students, the students would benefit. One of the most perplexing concerns for her was why so many administrators keep some data "secret." She asked teachers to share questions or concerns about this topic in a brainstorming session.
>
> The most frequently cited concern related to supply budgets. Why does every teacher get the same amount? Isn't there a difference in the instructional supply needs across disciplines? Many teachers wanted to know what the budget was for all the needs in the school. Why was all this information kept "secret"?
>
> The new principal talked with other principals and two of her former professors. The only conclusion she could reach was that not sharing the budget was perceived as a form of responsibility and control. So she established a budget committee whose responsibility was to draft procedures for budget information and allocation based on teachers' established needs. This was new data for these teachers.
>
> What, if any, data should be secret? (Hint: one area is personnel evaluations.)

of teachers and staff to give you regular feedback (often the role of a leadership team) on specific questions. Or you could create simple surveys using one of the many freely available survey tools on the Internet, such as SurveyMonkey (2010) or Zoomerang (2010). Because you need well-developed surveys if you are going to get the information you need to make changes, the authors encourage you to do some research or take a course on developing surveys or hire a professional to do the job. Some of the software systems, like Smart-Survey (2011), have easy-to-read explanations of the procedure. Now you know why those college professors made you take that research course, don't you?!

Figure 4.1 can give you quick feedback on the school's attempts to achieve a specific goal.

This survey will allow you to consider the progress and areas for improvement of both the principal and the teachers in their attempts to achieve a defined goal. This information can be compiled and analyzed (formally or informally) to help you identify the things you should celebrate about your school, the things that are going well for both principal and teachers, and then fine-tune or revise the steps toward the goal as called for in an analysis of the identified areas of improvement.

Gathering data to address team functioning can provide very helpful information. Strategies for examining a team include assessing the context in which the work is to occur, the desired results, the purpose of the team, the people involved, the structure and resources of the team, and the strategies and skills required (see York-Barr, Sommerness, & Hur, 2008).

A very useful strategy that a principal can use to figure out what's happening in a school involves three simple questions: *What's working? What are your issues and concerns? What would be your ideal teaching and learning environment?* To gather this data, the principal can meet with each teaching team (grade level or department) and the staff (office, custodians, cafeteria) as individual groups. Then he can collate the responses and bring larger groups together (e.g., multiple grades or disciplines, all staff) to examine the collated responses, eliminate duplicates, and add anything participants felt was missing, repeating this step with the entire school. Once this process is completed, the faculty and staff can celebrate "what's working" by choosing comments at random to share in the weekly faculty/staff newsletter.

The last and most important step is to deal with the problems that the survey identified. To narrow down the number of "issues and concerns," the

Figure 4.1 Goal Survey

Things the principal is doing well to achieve our goal of improving student engagement in math:
Things the principal could improve to achieve our goal of improving student engagement in math:
Things I am doing well to achieve our goal of improving student engagement in math:
Things I could improve to achieve our goal of improving student engagement in math:

principal can use the nominal technique (page 22) and perform an N/4 to prioritize the issues and identify a starting place. It is important to assure teachers and staff that all issues and concerns will be addressed while reminding them that you have to start "someplace." You can establish priorities by listing all the issues on chart paper and discussing them in a faculty meeting, or you can enter the issues in an electronic survey tool and ask teachers to identify their individual top concerns through that mechanism. In either event, the number of issues and concerns that each individual gets to identify is based on the number determined by the N/4 procedure.

As an example, let's assume there are twenty-four issues (there will almost always be more issues and concerns than responses to either of the other two questions). Dividing 24 by 4 equals 6. So each faculty and staff member is asked to choose six issues by checking them off either on the chart paper or the online survey. You can thus quickly see what most faculty and staff members consider the top issues. Be sure that you know *all* the identified issues and assure faculty and staff that work will begin to address the top issues first. Your next task will involve deciding with whom to work to address the issues and concerns.

Observing Teachers

A lot of research indicates that the teacher is the person who exerts the most influence on a student's performance level. Also, the best teachers "rapidly alternate between teaching and questioning or otherwise testing. Poor performers (teachers) drone on for a long time and then let the students struggle, often leaving students to repeat the same errors" (Patterson et al., 2008). When you read that statement, you probably thought of one of your worst teachers, who lectures to the class for hours on end and whose students' test scores are mediocre at best. Let's put that same concept another way: can you think of a *great* teacher who simply lectures all day and only gives summative assessments? Probably not. It takes a combination of techniques to ensure learning on the part of each student. No one method works for all students.

Perhaps you have already recognized that there is a problem with "the lecturer" and thought about how to change that teacher's behavior with little success. The key question: What data do you have that will help you make decisions about what *specific teacher behaviors* need to be changed? Simply providing teachers with a review of their poor test scores, their "final score," isn't going to be enough to change their teaching styles. You also can't simply say to the teacher "You lecture too much" and expect that alone will solve the problem. You have to get your poor teachers to start thinking differently about how they teach, and administrators have to start thinking differently about how they access and use data to positively influence how teachers teach. Patterson et al. (2008) make a strong argument:

> Take care to ensure that you're searching for strategies that focus on behavior. . . . Master influencers know that a few behaviors can drive big change. They look carefully for the vital behaviors that create a cascade of change. No matter the size of the problem, if you dilute your efforts across dozens of behaviors, you'll never reach critical mass. Look for people, times, or places where you or others don't experience the same problems and try to determine the unique differences that make the difference. (p. 43)

Most principals go through the practice of observing classrooms at random, using a standard observation form. They check off a list of items on the form and then leave it with the teacher. Too often principals do not follow up on their observations to provide specific feedback, but more importantly they're not looking for something specific when they walk into the classroom. If principals know that rapidly alternating between teaching and questioning is a strategy that works for successful teachers, then why aren't we looking for that specific behavior when we do classroom observations? If we know that a lack of engagement (making sure there's a clear understanding of that concept in a school) is a problem, then why aren't we observing for engagement specifically–and nothing else—when we do classroom observations?

Just as annual test scores supply information about students, summative assessment data about teachers will provide you with a starting point—but that's about it. This information will show you where you have strengths and weaknesses in your building. It will tell you where to look for the teaching strategies that work and it may indicate some curriculum weaknesses and strengths. Most of the schools in this nation have at least one master teacher whom you can observe in order to find out what strategies are working. The most effective use of your time is observing great teachers to determine what they're doing that's different from what less successful teachers are doing. From there, your job is to create an observation form to target those specific behaviors. This task can be done most effectively when you include teachers and a leadership team in sharing and modeling exactly what those teaching strategies are.

Step 1: In a collaborative effort with teachers in your building, identify the strategies in your building that are the most effective. Douglas Reeves (2010) has created professional development videos specific to this process.

Step 2: Create an observation form that will allow you to gather data specific to those strategies across your building. It's important that you also create a systematic process and schedule for doing classroom observations (along with your team).

Step 3: Analyze your data after a set period of time. Determine which teachers are the least likely and the most likely to use the successful strategy. These data should be used to target professional development.

Step 4: Create a professional development plan to help your weakest teachers learn the successful strategy. Communicate to them how you plan to monitor their progress.

Step 5: Monitor the progress of teachers, providing specific feedback at least weekly. It would be highly beneficial to have teachers monitor their own progress as well!

Regardless of the way in which you collect data, it is valuable to remember that no one person is capable of identifying everything that is needed to ensure a positive, productive learning environment. A new approach has teachers observe each other on targeted strategies and discuss their problems and successes (see Chapter 6 on professional learning). Likewise, administrators have a view of the school and its needs, but so do students and teachers. If you are aware of your own strengths and weaknesses in leading and developing others, you can draw on the strengths of others to help lead various initiatives.

Knowing Yourself

"Throughout, leaders need to be aware and awake: consciousness accelerates development. The greater the awareness, the faster the growth. It also extracts more meaning from the journey's experience" (Henein & Morissette, 2007). The role of leader is not bound to position. Although many leadership theories espouse a positional framework, "the executive leader," leadership requires followership. In 2006 the US Tennis Association renamed its famous public courts in New York City the USTA Billie Jean King National Tennis Center. In a television interview, King was asked if she knew when she was nine and already a great tennis player that she would end up being the national leader that she became. She answered, "Leaders do not choose their followers; followers choose their leaders." It is a well-learned lesson when realizing that while individual effort can result in accomplishments, leadership exists only when there are others who follow you. In education, the quality of leadership must also be considered to ensure that the leadership is focused on the most important aspect of schools: student learning.

The very hierarchical nature of public schools, even in 2012, is strongly rooted in positional power. Boards tell superintendents what to do, superintendents tell principals, principals tell teachers, and teachers tell students. Like the instructions on the shampoo bottle, mentioned in Chapter 1, this scenario of positional power is repeated day after day in schools across the land. But there is a difference between positional power and leadership. Positional power grants you the authority to make decisions on behalf of the organization, as defined by the position. However, position does not ensure leadership. As Billie Jean King stated, leadership requires followers.

Why is this important? How does it relate to "understanding self"? Is it possible to "understand self"? You can examine these weighty questions in the context of what you do by attending various workshops on strategies for examining your leadership style. Which one you attend is not as important as knowing *why* you should go through such an exercise. There are strengths and weaknesses to all such inventories and assessments, but the important reason for doing one is to determine, on some measure or scale, the way you "think" or "act." For example, the Life Styles Inventory (LSI) (Human Synergistics Lab 2011) requires you to get feedback from others to provide some perspective for your personal assessment.

Another leadership assessment, available online, is the MLQ30 Management & Leadership Test (2011). Although this assessment has a number of questions with a business focus, it draws on the literature in leadership that makes it applicable to leadership regardless of the field in which you work. It provides a multidimensional framework of competencies in both leadership and management. When Jacque took the inventory, it showed her as "likely to be very effective in situations where a transformational leader is required to deliver change" and "likely to be reasonably effective in situations where a person is required with good management skills." This is a fairly accurate assessment. She can "do" the management tasks, but much prefers the developmental work that leads others toward transforming the environment, in this case the student learning environment, over the management side of things.

The authors have also used the Leadership Compass (2011) with many pre-service and in-service principals over the last six or seven years. This instrument, which you can do on your own, uses the Native American practice known as the Medicine Wheel or Four-Fold Way. Each of the four major points on the compass is identified with specific attributes, their uses and overuses. Going through the exercise helps you determine which compass direction is your primary place of action. Those with whom the authors have done this exercise have repeatedly commented that it was one of the most meaningful things they have done to understand themselves.

Regardless of the instrument used, the focus should be on understanding who you are and what is called your "default" mode of operating at any given time. The reason you need to know your default, whether authoritarian, collaborative, or one of the directions, such as "north-warrior" or "south-healer," is that those characteristics are the position from which you will act in crisis. If, for instance, Jacque is truly a transformational leader, as identified in the survey mentioned above, then in a crisis such as a fire in the school building, she is much more likely to think about the needs of the people involved than about the damage to the facility. Although she will manage things related to the facility, she will put much more energy into serving the needs of the people affected by the fire. Jacque knows that about herself and the trait was validated in taking the inventory online.

You will note that the definition of *default* above states, "mode of operating at any given time." Does the given point in time matter? Yes! Because each of us is capable of learning and growing in our leadership style, just as principals need to help teachers in their journey to grow as leaders of learning.

Drawing Conclusions: Validating the Need for Change

In the twenty-first century, principals often feel inundated with many kinds of data, such as benchmarks and state and national test scores. Clearly, these data are important. But the most important consideration is how the principal *uses* the data. Inevitably, conclusions are drawn from data and it is important to put that research course from your graduate education to use. Graduate students often ask, "Why do we need to take a research course?" How could they not? If, as a principal, you have collected data or plan to collect additional data, you have to know how to analyze and use that data, as well as what you *know* and *don't know* based on the data.

The demands under state and federal legislation to test students annually and have those scores reported and used for determining the progress of instruction in a school are well known. In most states, however, those data are not meaningful at the individual student level. Most are not articulated from grade level to grade level and thus do not show individual student growth.

Do not make the mistake of concluding that these scores are irrelevant data; they are not. But their purpose provides only a look at the surface: the overall picture. The need to consider individual student achievement reminded Jacque of a personal story:

> Years ago my husband and I wanted to have a well dug on some land that we had purchased to build a new home just outside of town. Someone told us that we should have Mr. Jones divine our land to find the underground water source. Although we were skeptical, we decided it would be interesting as we had never seen anyone use this technique (old and tried as it was). Mr. Jones arrived in his truck with the Y-shaped tree branch that he used to search for water. With no more than a handshake with each of us, he walked off. Finally, he stopped as we watched the end of his stick point to the ground. He said, without fanfare, "Water's here. Twenty-five feet." My husband jokingly said, "Does that come with a guarantee?" Mr. Jones said, "Double or nothing if I hit at twenty-five." Sure enough, he hit water at twenty-five feet and a double water source at thirty-five feet. What does this little story have to do with annual testing data? Of all the land on the seven acres we had, Mr. Jones picked one spot to put a well. There could have been more places, for sure, but this spot was the target.

That's how educators use annual test data. If you see that 60 percent of your male African American students did not reach the proficient level on the end-of-grade math tests, should teachers focus on African American males as a group? Maybe the fact of being African American is a consideration in how a student scores, but maybe the huge overlap between the poverty level of those same students and their exposure to language and learning prior to entering school is also a factor. What do the 40 percent of African American males who are proficient or advanced have to say about their performance? What do the 60 percent of African American males who are not at the proficient level have to say? What could we learn from both groups about the math instruction in our school? Without the ability to measure individual student growth, educators will continue to be challenged to meet individual student learning needs.

As a principal, what data do you need in order to determine individual student growth? To draw conclusions about student learning and teacher performance? Many schools and districts have implemented different forms of benchmark testing, but do little to help teachers learn how to use the data to improve instruction. Let's think about formative assessments in categories that educators often confuse and use interchangeably—and often incorrectly.

Benchmark Assessments

Benchmark assessments are given throughout the school year at regularly set intervals to provide teachers with information about how an entire class or grade level is progressing toward grade-level content mastery. Shorter benchmark assessments may also be used to determine progress toward mastery of certain instructional units. In best practice, benchmark assessments have been studied to determine their reliability and validity. However, having teachers work locally in groups to develop a set of benchmark assessments specific to shared course standards they teach can help create a collaborative approach to addressing school needs. Besides influencing teachers in their

Sharing . . .

> Last summer Jacque took her thirteen-year-old great-nephew, Asher, to hear Hal Herzog talk about his recent book *Some We Love, Some We Hate, Some We Eat: Why It's So Hard to Think Straight About Animals* (2010). Herzog cited a well-known writer on vegetarianism who said there are more vegetarians in the United States today than there were thirty years ago. Herzog also showed a graph indicating that the percentage of vegetarians in the country has remained at 4 percent.
>
> After the talk, Jacque asked Asher if it was possible for both things to be true: that more people are vegetarians and that the percentage of the vegetarian population was still about 4 percent. We agreed that one statement implies growth and the other consistency. After thinking a bit, he said, "Does it have to do with there being more people now than thirty years ago? So there could be more actual people who are vegetarians, but the larger population would mean the percentage of people hasn't changed." WOW! He got it!
>
> Try posing the question to your teachers at a faculty meeting. It might be interesting to see how many figure it out.
>
> If they can solve this simple problem, then you are ahead of the game on getting them to truly examine what data they need to improve student learning!

instructional practice, benchmark assessment results should also drive the professional development that the school provides to teachers.

The term *local assessment* simply means that the assessment was created by a group of local educators. Local assessments are typically developed to provide teachers with specific information about the topics that they are teaching. Local assessments can be formative or summative. Local assessment *data*, however, refers to data from various assessments that apply to a specific school or location.

Common Assessments

Common assessments are assessments that are given to groups of students taking the same course, but not necessarily from the same teacher. For example, all Algebra I teachers in a school district may give the same benchmark or final exam to their students. People often use this term for assessments that are created locally in a collaborative effort by groups of educators. These assessments could be formative or summative. Arranging for teachers to work collaboratively to develop local common assessments is a powerful way to make progress in student achievement, especially when results from those assessments are used as the basis of conversations about the strategies used in individual teachers' classrooms that they believe had the most positive impact on student learning.

If you enter the classrooms where such data are available, what would you expect to see? Would student learning look different in a classroom without data? How?

Perhaps information on students is something that you have in abundance. However, the uses of that data may need to be examined. Educators collect many categories of student data without really knowing why. For instance, we know how students are identified by race, gender, and socioeconomic levels. However, in a very diverse society such as ours, race alone may have little relevance from a cultural or an ethnic perspective. For example, many educators assume that all students listed as "white/Caucasian" are similar. However, that is hardly true at even the most rudimentary levels. Certainly categories like birth order, number of siblings, religion, and educational background of parents can differ widely across the group of white/Caucasian students. Ultimately, the most important data we can have on students is individual growth in the learning environment. That is really all that matters.

In the mid-twentieth century it was not uncommon for professionals to talk about the importance of teacher judgment related to a student's performance. Today, after more than a half-century of standardized testing influencing public education, teacher judgment is not as commonly regarded as valuable as it once was. Why not? Most people still believe that teachers can influence a student's performance through their beliefs about the student, so why do we fail to use teacher judgment when designing instruction? Consider the teachers that you observe to be the most competent in student learning. What data do they use to assess student performance and how do they modify instruction as a result?

Another area of data from which conclusions are often drawn is student participation in activities. It is often reported that students who are involved in sports or other activities are more successful academically than students who do not participate in such activities. But the topic may need to be examined from the other side. Of those students who are not involved in sports or other activities but are successful academically, what are the factors that contribute to their success? There is a tried-and-true maxim among researchers: Correlation is not causation. Just because two things are related does not mean that one causes the other. Yet far too often, even educated people accept such statements of relationship with little thought about what the data are or what they mean.

Wrapping It Up

Assessments will have the most positive impact on student achievement when we quit using their results as a whipping post for educators. As instructional leaders, we must create opportunities for teachers to have productive conversations about assessment results so that the data shape instructional practice. We should also provide teachers with professional learning opportunities so they can learn how to have these conversations in a beneficial manner.

The bottom line in understanding the data you have and developing new data rests with knowing why you need to collect data and what you will do with it. Principals cannot all be experts at assessment, but you should know enough to ask the right questions and find someone, such as a district research consultant, who can help you develop the instrumentation to gather the data and, if needed, can help you interpret it. Data are important and useful in improving the quality of the learning environment and student engagement in learning. Use them wisely.

USING WHAT YOU'VE LEARNED

The following activity, conducted with your faculty and staff, will help you think about the kinds of data that are rarely, if ever, collected and yet can have profound influence on who we are.

When faculty and staff members enter the meeting area, have the following posted:

1. What is your birth order? (only child, oldest, middle, youngest)
2. Write two or three advantages of your birth order.
3. Write two or three disadvantages of your birth order.

Allow participants about five minutes to write their answers.

Write each of the headings "Only," "Youngest," "Middle," and "Oldest" on a separate large piece of chart paper and ask the participants to form groups under the appropriate headings. Then have each group come to consensus on three advantages and three disadvantages of their birth order. (Note: The authors' experience is that you will have more middle and/or youngest children than only and oldest children. So you may need to have multiple sheets if there are more than eight or ten people in a group.)

Lastly, have each group describe their advantages and then their disadvantages. Lead a discussion about how birth order is information that applies to everybody but is rarely considered because we don't collect the data. How might it influence what we know about our students?

5

Developing Habits of Thinking

Much of the work of leading learning in a school is challenged by the need to understand that each person has individual ways of thinking about the work. Over the years educators have heard many lectures, read many articles, and yes, even lived the language of shared decision making. But perhaps one of the main reasons that shared decision making is challenging is that educators rarely take the time to think about what they believe and why they do what they do, much less to think about how and why they think as they do. In this chapter, the authors will discuss the importance of developing beneficial habits of thinking.

Habits of Thinking: New Ideas or Old Baggage?

A bus is a bus is a bus. Right? An assistant principal (AP) felt that one of her greatest challenges was the number of discipline referrals from bus drivers, particularly from the afternoon runs. On a visit to her school, Jacque observed the bus dismissal routine, which the AP oversees. Here is what she saw: eight buses, lined up, with their engines running for twenty-four minutes; students behaving in an orderly fashion while exiting the building and getting on the buses; students yelling to their friends on the buses over the noise of the bus engines.

When the buses left, Jacque asked, "What did you see?" The AP replied, "Routine dismissal. All buses here on time, students loaded in normal time, buses didn't have to wait for anyone, all buses pulled out in order. What did you see?" Jacque said, "(1) I saw buses burning fuel for twenty-four minutes—what does that cost? (2) I saw buses idling, which are more likely to slip into gear than buses with the engines off—that's dangerous. (3) I saw students shouting to be heard by their friends over the engine noise, which certainly could contribute to bus referrals. Is there one simple thing to do that would address all three of these problems?" The AP said, "Yes! We could turn off the bus engines, which would save fuel and minimize danger; starting the buses could be the signal for students to limit themselves to talking to their seat partners."

> What habits of thinking did we each exhibit when observing the same phenomenon? Does it matter if your "habit of thinking" focuses on solutions?

One of the great professional benefits for the authors of this book has been the opportunity to explore ideas and beliefs together. In one conversation, Jacque relayed the story about the buses to a colleague, saying, "How could I stand there and look at what was happening and identify a potential cause of the problems on the afternoon bus runs that end in student referrals, as well as see two other possible concerns: cost of fuel and potential danger?" She went on to say, "I don't think that I was ever taught in my leadership preparation to think about why I do what I do. I do think my father, who wanted me to be an engineer, taught me to think logically. But that kind of logic was not specific to my field."

Jacque and her colleague discussed the habits of thinking that people bring to situations. It is natural for people to draw on what they know, have experienced, or believe based on prior situations. When she was a new principal, Jacque was often surprised that teachers would say things to her like "I know that we can't do this, but I wanted to ask anyway . . . " or "Can I have permission to leave as soon as students are dismissed today?" These are not "essential questions" (Clifford & Friesen, 2007) in the sense of problem-solving the challenges of a productive learning environment for students, but the underlying reasons for the questions might be important for understanding the habits of thinking that teachers have in your school.

To consider your own operational level when it comes to determining how you think, what your individual habits of thinking are, so that you understand yourself as a leader, you need to have a basic understanding of your own responses to the following questions. Write your answers to these questions or, better yet, record yourself answering them on camera.

- What is my first reaction when I encounter a new situation?
- What is my first reaction when I encounter a problem?
- What is my first reaction when I have time to think of new ideas?

Once you've answered the questions for yourself (that is, once you've set the baseline of your thinking), the authors suggest that you begin to address your individual habits of thinking. One way to begin this is to go back and study your facial features and mannerisms in the recording. Try to imagine how others would perceive your responses. The following points are important in order to understanding habits of thinking and to developing new ones.

Using Essential Questions to Differentiate Symptoms from Problems

"Essential questions develop foundational understandings. They provide the fundamental organizing principles that bound an inquiry and guide the development of meaningful, authentic tasks" (Clifford & Friesen, 2007). While all the things that occur in a given day at school certainly do not rise to the level of identifying the essential questions of life, if we don't know how to ask probing questions, we won't know how to search for answers.

An effective principal will push teachers to identify a problem when they want to focus on the symptoms. The principal does this by asking essential questions. For example, a student is sent to the office for being out of her seat without the teacher's permission. In a conversation with the teacher, the principal says, "So what's the problem?" "Janie's out of her seat." "That's a symptom—why is she out of her seat?" "She won't do her work." "That's a symptom—why won't she do her work?" And while this exchange may continue with the description of more and more symptoms, the teacher ultimately ends up with "Janie can't read the material." Ah . . . now we know the problem.

Creating a solution that is likely to impact all the symptoms is now possible because the underlying problem, that Janie can't do the work she's being assigned, has been identified. Too often, teachers are quick to focus on the symptoms because the symptoms are present, real, and obvious, but a solution that merely addresses the symptoms rarely succeeds because we haven't identified the underlying problem by asking essential questions.

The Attitude of Questioning

When you read the heading "Attitude of Questioning," you may have thought, "Oh, yeah, he sure has an attitude every time he asks a question!" or perhaps, "Her attitude is to question everything!" or even, "What in the world does 'attitude of questioning' mean?" No matter what reaction the phrase generated for you, if any at all, the authors want you to consider that one challenge for educators is their willingness to spend the time to develop an attitude of questioning. As a child, perhaps you were always in trouble for asking questions such as *Why? What for? When will we know? What does it really look like? Can I do that? Who said that's wrong?* Yes, questioning may come naturally to some of us, but it is more and more apparent in this increasingly complex world that we have to teach our students to ask questions, not just answer them.

Sharing . . .

> Developing skill in the use of essential questions requires practice. One way to gain that practice is to take each of the following statements and either role-play them with someone else or write out the questions and possible responses so you can examine them.
>
> 1. Based on multiple drop-in visits to a classroom, you find that students are sleeping during class time. You set up a meeting to talk with the teacher. What questions will you ask?
> 2. In reviewing your discipline data, you examine the referrals by teacher and find that 60 percent of the discipline referrals in your school originate with six teachers. You plan to meet with your assistant principal and try to develop a strategy to address this situation. What questions will you raise to figure out how and with whom you will work to determine the underlying problem?
> 3. A teacher comes to you to discuss the new Common Core State Standards because she doesn't want to do "one more thing" the "district" says she has to do. What questions will you ask to understand the problem underlying her objection?

Questioning, long the purview of the teacher, has been used to determine the acquisition of knowledge and skills among the students. And more often than not, expectations were that there would be a "right" answer. Just as teachers are asked to utilize Bloom's revised taxonomy (Anderson, Krathwohl, & Bloom, 2001) in the cognitive aspects of learning, a principal can consider the kinds of issues in the day-to-day running of a school that are addressed by different levels of the cognitive taxonomy as a way of examining how to question, thus think, about one's actions (see Figure 5.1).

As a first-year principal, Jacque was not a typical appointee. She had been an ELA teacher, a teacher of students with learning disabilities and/or behavior disorders, a special education coordinator, a special education director, and a professor of special education. She was very glad she had had those opportunities because within her first month as principal, she faced three major crises and one minor but painful one: a fifth grader was raped on the way home from school, a kindergartner's finger was severed in the bathroom door, the school resource officer was arrested for grand theft, and Jacque caught shingles from a prekindergartner who was so unsettled during nap time that she carried him to her office and rocked him until he fell asleep.

She had no experience with any of these specific events. But she was able to draw on her level of *understanding* of crisis situations in general and *apply* what she knew from her previous work with students with behavior disorders and from the theory she had learned in her principal preparation program. Based on the actions taken, she later made notes for herself as a way of *analyzing* the situation (which the leadership team also did) and then talked with others to determine their analysis of each of the situations; together they *evaluated* their procedures. Based on this evaluation, they determined if they needed to *create* any new procedures or practices.

Clearly, not all situations are crises, but some become crises because we fail to think about—or ask the right questions about—the data that are often right in front of us. And the conditions of society today demand that we educate children and young people to think, a process that, by its very nature, involves questioning.

In a 2007 article in *BusinessWeek*, Brian Hindo reported a conflict facing the century-old company 3M between its vaunted practice of allowing time for employees to think and create and its need to be efficient and generate profits. Systems that generate efficiency inherently focus on time management and productivity. Innovation is a disorderly process, as Hindo noted in his discussion of George Buckley, 3M's CEO: "While process excellence demands precision, consistency, and repetition, innovation calls for variation, failure, and serendipity" (p. 10).

Figure 5.1 Modeling Bloom's Revised Taxonomy

Level of questioning	Example of actions taken by a principal	Identify some of your own actions
Remember (knowledge)	Where to find district crisis plans	
Understand (comprehension)	Actions to take in a dangerous situation	
Apply	Acting on understanding of a situation being dangerous	
Analyze	Review actions taken and procedures or policies after the crisis	
Evaluate	Determine strengths and weaknesses of actions taken and procedures or policies identified in analysis	
Create (synthesis)	Brainstorm ways to revise	

The disorder that comes with innovation is similar to the disorder that can occur in schools when people question the status quo, when they don't challenge the status quo, or when teachers are challenged to think about the changes needed in educating children and young people today. So it is important that principals develop a school culture that highlights an attitude of questioning. This will often require planning and deliberate development to ensure that the efforts are focused on the identified objective (e.g., new teaching strategies, senior projects).

The Attitude of Reflection

Comments often come quickly from principals and superintendents when faced with the challenge to take time to reflect. "I wish I had time to reflect," they say; "I can't even think straight enough some days to reflect." Reflection is not just thinking about what happened. Reflection is thinking about where you want to be . . . what outcome would have been more desirable . . . what outcome would have been more effective.

A principal intern, during the course of her first-semester internship, delivered a baby who died thirteen days later. When she returned to her internship the following semester, she was challenged to focus on her work—teaching, leading the school improvement team, continuing graduate study with extensive field-based learning—while she was still grieving. Her principal gave her a beautifully bound journal and encouraged her to write three things that she could celebrate each day: "a beautiful sunny day"; "my four-year-old ran up to me today and said, 'Mommy, I love you *this* much' while stretching her arms out as wide as she could"; "a student who had worked hard to understand the concept of numeracy had a breakthrough today." Each of these is a reflection. Granted, her principal had guided her toward focusing on something positive so she could find a way to refocus herself in her time of grief. Writing in the journal helped her develop a new practice in her personal and professional life: a habit of reflection.

Principals can choose a focus for reflection: personal or professional. It is through reflection, both our own and the feedback provided by others (another form of reflection), that we can examine our work and its effect on other people. The reflection is not sufficient unto itself. We must use reflection to improve our own actions, to enhance the milieu in which we work, and to ensure that the focus of our work remains on our students, even when most of the contacts of a principal or superintendent are with the adults in the environment.

Surveying Those Affected

As part of developing habits of thinking, including questioning and reflecting, it is safe to assume that our own behaviors are affected by our actions of thinking, questioning, and reflecting. However, we can only truly know if they impact our work and that of others if we are willing to ask. Many states have implemented an annual or biannual statewide system of surveying teachers and parents. In North Carolina, for example, the survey for teachers is known as the *Teacher Working Conditions Survey*. It is assumed that principals and superintendents will use the survey information to assess what is happening in their schools, as perceived by the teachers, and address those needs and concerns. These data are public.

While annual data are important and there is some merit in having a common measure across schools in a district or state, principals can easily do their own quick survey of teachers as a way of collecting formative data that will allow you to monitor and adjust your path in a given year. (Be sure you know your district's policy on conducting teacher surveys.) Your survey can be as simple as a conversation with several employees, individually or collectively; you can also use an anonymous survey instrument.

Whatever format you choose for surveying your faculty members to determine professional growth and their progress toward identifying or identified goals, it is important to determine (survey) what they observe, see, and believe about that growth or progress or need. Obtaining feedback will help you assess whether you are asking the right questions and thus correctly identifying the problems for which you are seeking to create solutions.

Using the information you acquire from teacher/parent/student surveys can either enhance or reinforce your habits of thinking. If you adopt the attitude that you need this information to help the school reach the next step on the way to a specific goal, you will be more likely to be objective about the information garnered. Chapter 4, for example, presented the Leadership Compass. If you are predominantly a "north," you are likely to be analytical and consider each survey question relative to what needs to be done to address the responses. If you tend to be a "south," you are likely to be somewhat more emotional in your reading of the survey responses because your tendency to be a nurturer makes the responses feel more personal.

Let's take an example of a district or state survey that provides information from your teachers. Depending on how the questions are organized and phrased, the focus may be on matters that the administrator supervises rather than what she does in her specific role. The authors suggest using the following strategy to think about the survey results.

First, create a document labeled something like "Survey initial response." Second, read the survey results through completely. Third, write your initial response. This can contain all the emotion you may experience as well as your analysis. Just write! Then walk away for an hour or more. Fourth, return to the survey results and start to analyze them. Consider that a negative response may not be all bad. Perhaps you are trying to develop a new system that will help teachers use data in their instructional design. Your efforts may result in some pushback from some teachers. Look at the percentage of respondents compared to the number of teachers in the school. Then look at the percentage of negative responses. This kind of critical analysis can help you get perspective.

Once you have analyzed the responses to the survey, you will want to share the analysis with the teachers and staff so they know that you are serious about addressing their concerns and celebrating what is going well in your school. A note of caution about glowing surveys: if everyone in the survey rates you highly on every question, it may be because your school is a "congenial" school, as described by Glickman, Gordon, and Ross-Gordon (2004). While the positive results allow you to celebrate the congenial atmosphere you have established, you may need to consider how you are going to move toward a school where student learning is the focus and where there may be some unsettled people as you move new ideas forward.

The emphasis here is not on surveys or even on the results. It is on what you do with the results. What are your habits of thinking relative to information you receive about the teaching and learning in your school?

Wrapping It Up

It may be when we no longer know what to do
We have come to our real work,
And when we no longer know which way to go,
We have begun our real journey.
The mind that is not baffled is not employed.
The impeded stream is the one that sings.

—Wendell Berry

The following short examples may help you think about why asking the right questions and developing habits of thinking and reflecting are important. While Jacque was working as a district's consultant, a principal happily shared his observation form with her, which included a place to check whether standards and indicators were posted in the classroom. He stated that 98 percent of the times he entered classrooms, the standards and indicators were posted." Jacque said, "Great! Now take it to the next level." He said, "Do you mean I should demand 100 percent?" She said, "Well, clearly, having standards posted daily in 100 percent of the classrooms can be a goal. But how do you know if the standards and indicators being posted make a difference to the learners?" He said, "I have no idea." So Jacque and the principal talked about randomly asking students in a class how what they were doing related to the standards posted on the wall. The principal had a focus: getting the standards posted. When challenged to think beyond that, he was able to see that the purpose for posting the standards and indicators was to enhance student learning.

A high-school principal thought that her observation checklist had become stilted and was not getting at the heart of the instructional concerns she had related to student learning. Jacque asked some essential questions: "What is your goal in doing classroom walk-throughs?" "To see what's happening in the classrooms." "What does that mean?" "Well, you know, is the teacher teaching and are the students learning?" "How do you know if they are learning? *What* they are learning?" "I don't know that I do know. I think I just assume that if the teacher is not behind her desk and is either lecturing or talking with students and the kids appear to be listening, then it's good teaching and learning. So you see my dilemma." That led to a discussion about the purpose of class time. What are the outcomes expected of the students? How will the teacher know if a student already had achieved those outcomes before the class started? How will the teacher know if the student reaches those outcomes as a result of the class? The principal realized that changes in instructional practices take conversation. Change takes questioning and reflection.

The same concepts are true in working with teachers. Do teachers know what is expected of them? How? Do they know what outcomes are expected? Do they know how the outcomes are measured? Do you, as the principal, know what the teachers already know about your goals for students? What they don't know? Not knowing is, as Wendell Berry states, when "we have come to our real work."

USING WHAT YOU'VE LEARNED

Go back to your responses to the bulleted questions at the beginning of this chapter (page 66). Now consider what you have read in this chapter and identify two or three people you can trust and will be comfortable talking with about your responses (e.g., teachers, other administrators in similar roles to yours, spouse, friends). Set up times to talk with those people about your responses. After each person has read your responses, ask:

1. How does he or she think you would react in each situation? Does this match your written responses?
2. If so, does he or she think you would be reacting appropriately?
3. If not, how does he or she think you would actually react?

The purpose here is to get perspective on your habits of thinking.

6

Professional Learning: Development of Self and Others

With the increased demands for student learning at grade level in each subject, there is no doubt that teachers have to add to their knowledge base of content, as well as meet the ever-changing demands for finding ways to engage students in learning. There has long been a belief that "professional development" (PD) comes only from attending workshops, lectures, university classes, and so on. Over the last decade, professional learning communities (PLC) have become more popular, but they, like too many PD sessions, are often set up with little attention to the outcomes and intended purpose other than "professional growth." In this chapter, the authors will examine some of the purposes of professional learning, some types of professional learning that are important to consider, and a brief overview of the reasons for professional learning that can assist you in considering the needs in your school. For an in-depth look at professional learning, including types, standards, and ways to evaluate it, the authors recommend Sally Zepeda's *Professional Development: What Works*, Second Edition (2012).

The authors are purposely using the term *professional learning* instead of the historic term *professional development* because they believe it embraces the concept of learning for teachers and administrative leaders, as well as the students they serve.

The Purposes of Professional Learning

Working with a group of principals, Jacque was asked by a very bright and dedicated second-year principal, "How do I talk with a teacher after my class visits?" He had already led many positive changes in his first year as principal. His desire to make the meeting with the teachers instructionally meaningful was evident. He had also shared the new mission they had developed for the school and said he wanted to be able to address students who were not making satisfactory progress in learning.

Reflecting . . .

> "I can't tell you how many times I have attended staff learning with absolutely no follow-up or expectations for implementation and the entire training was just a wash. I like the quote from the article, 'Staff development is important because it can help educators prepare themselves and enlist the support of their colleagues to change what they think, what they do, and how they do it to benefit the education of the students' (Mizell, 2002, p. 151). I think as future administrators, we have to keep our eyes on that goal. Staff learning should be for the purposes of helping teachers help students. It has to be real and useful, not just a time filler" (M. Jacobs, 2010).
>
> The future administrator who posted this in a discussion board of an online class has challenged all of us to consider our roles as teachers and administrators. What *do* we expect the outcome of professional learning to be? Have we identified the desired outcomes of the professional learning? Do we know what we will see as a result of the professional learning?

Jacque asked him what he does after his walk-throughs. He said, "Well, I use the checklist I take with me and share that with them and tell them what I observed." He thought the check sheet was only helping him to get the "obvious" things, like standards posted, indicators posted, and student actions. So she said, "What if you asked these three questions, giving the teacher time to respond after each:

1. What do you think was the best thing about what was occurring in your lesson when I was in the room?
2. If you could change one thing about the lesson, what would it be?
3. Let's look at Student X (pick a student at random) from third period. Tell me about this student's progress toward reaching our stated mission for "college-ready" students. How can we help this student on that path?"

Once the teacher has addressed these questions, the principal can enter into dialogue with the teacher. One of the reasons that so many principals avoid classroom visits is that they are afraid they will appear ignorant of the content or strategies that the teacher is using. This fear is pointless: no one person can be an expert in every aspect of teaching or content. However, listening to teachers talk about the learning of their students and their instruction can help you, as the principal, know what the teachers need and want in terms of professional learning and can actually become part of your own professional learning as the leader of learning. When you visit classrooms as a regular part of your week, you quickly can identify the experts in your own school who can help other teachers. It seems obvious that visiting classes with a purposeful intent to learn can help teachers grow as well.

If you go back and look at the three "simple" questions on page 76, you can consider the profound effect they might have on the professional learning of the teacher. By asking teachers to analyze their teaching, the principal moves from the sole role of evaluator to the role of developer. The teachers are (or must be) the experts in their subject content and strategies. If you allow yourself to move to the role of coach, you can help others to become winners. Sally Zepeda (2008) offers excellent suggestions and in-depth explanations on different types of coaching and how to use them.

It is difficult for teachers to see themselves and their relationship to the learning environment because they are integral to it. However, when a principal or another teacher observes classrooms as a leader of student learning and invites the teachers to talk about what they are doing, they can develop the skill of being more analytical about their teaching. When teachers get feedback based on what they thought was going on and how it was observed by someone else, they have an opportunity to grow.

Clearly, individual teacher growth is an important outcome of professional learning. Later on in this chapter, the authors address improving the performance of teachers whose performance is marginal. Sometimes principals just fail to consider that teachers, like their students, think differently, act differently, and need to be taught differently, too.

A high-school assistant principal was intrigued by the fact that most of her teachers' professional learning revolved around classroom management strategies, that disciplinary referrals seemed to come from the same few teachers repeatedly, and that she spent a lot of time on the students who were referred, but none on helping the teachers learn how to keep students engaged in class so they could learn. After reading about Glickman, Gordon, and Ross-Gordon's (2004) "teacher types" (professional, analytical thinker, unfocused worker, and dropout), she started to consider differentiating classroom management based on the teacher types and student referral rates. With her principal's approval, she categorized each teacher in the school according to one of Glickman's types and examined the referral data against the teacher types. She thought that the most referrals would be from teachers who were identified as dropouts, but, interestingly, the most referrals actually came from teachers identified as unfocused workers. She then set up professional learning groups based on the teacher types (without revealing these criteria to the teachers):

1. The professional teachers, who overwhelmingly had the fewest referrals, addressed the school discipline policy as their professional learning.
2. The analytical thinkers focused on the disciplinary data and ways to reduce the number of referrals.
3. The unfocused workers, who made the most referrals in this particular school, received training based on how teacher-student relationships can benefit the teaching and learning environment.
4. The dropout teachers received training on specific strategies they could use to enforce the discipline code and expectations for their students and themselves.

The members of each professional learning group were thus engaged in an aspect of classroom management corresponding to the way they approached their profession.

As you can see from this example, differentiating the professional learning for teachers (regardless of the way in which you determine the need) is likely to address the way teachers approach student learning and their own way of performing. An added plus will eventually be that, if we differentiate their learning, they will start to differentiate for their students.

While the range of topics for professional learning is endless, not all professional learning comes from formally organized professional learning activities. Some occurs in a climate of discussion around learning. To ensure student learning, professional learning needs to be provided in ways that will meet the needs of your teachers in your school.

Where to Begin?

As Douglas Reeves (2010) states, "Focus is *the* 21st Century Learning skill." He points out that educators have become so accustomed to multitasking that they have lost the ability to focus in order to recognize problems, as well as the ability to solve those problems because their attention is so divided. How many times have you heard, or said yourself, that you do not have enough time to get everything done that needs to be done in a school day? How many fires do you put out in a day that keep you from actually accomplishing positive change in your educational setting? Do you focus on symptoms that you are trying to cure as opposed to the actual underlying problem? Have you applied so many Band-Aids to a gaping wound that you no longer see the actual problem—yet it still festers?

Too many principals take on every new instructional strategy or program they come across, hoping it will be the silver bullet they've been searching for to cure all their problems—although they are sometimes unsure of what their problems actually are. Principals "sell" these Band-Aids to their teachers, but all too often fail to explain how the new programs or strategies tie into the school's big picture—also known as a common vision (at least it's common if everyone shares it!). Teachers view the new strategies simply as "more work" that's being imposed on them as opposed to something they choose to incorporate into their classroom. In order to end this cycle of ineffective and inefficient professional learning, the principal needs to consider how to identify the needs of learners (both students and teachers), how to determine the topics to be covered in a given professional learning activity, and how to examine and/or evaluate the usefulness of the professional learning for teachers and, more importantly, for student learning.

The Needs of Learners

Begin with the end in mind! When making decisions about professional learning activities, you first have to know what those activities are supposed to accomplish. What is your school's mission? If you have a mission statement, are you sure that it's clear and up to date? Do your teachers understand the needs of parents and your community? What strategies will you employ to work with teachers who have marginal performance? It is doubtful that you alone know the answer to what your teachers are trying to accomplish, and even if you do, it is important that you lead teachers to a similar conclusion as opposed to telling them what it is.

Much like twenty-first-century students, teachers need to engage in collaborative discussions with their peers and other stakeholders in order to establish, or revisit, a common vision and goals for student achievement. You obviously could have other types of goals, such as environmental, social, or emotional, but ultimately your focus should be on student achievement and all that impacts learning. Principals should facilitate that process in an efficient manner (see the *Using What You've Learned* box at the end of this chapter).

Once you receive feedback from your faculty and other stakeholders about the specific needs for professional learning, it's imperative that a team or committee is formed to discuss specific professional learning activities that utilize strategies from the most recent research.

Sharing . . .

Formal professional learning activities best serve when the following questions are considered:

1. Is this professional learning most efficiently delivered as a group activity? For example, orienting everyone to a new program, procedure, strategy, curriculum, or text is an appropriate group activity.
2. Does everyone need to attend? What is the content? Which teachers need the content? Can you preassess to determine who needs to attend?
3. How will you assess use or implementation of the professional learning? Will those who attend be required to demonstrate the knowledge or strategy in the classroom? Will those who attend be required to share it with others on the faculty?
4. What outcomes are expected from the professional learning? Specific goals will be written with "look for" actions on the part of the teachers as a result of the training.

Teachers will observe each other as fidelity checks on implementing the content or strategy.

The Appropriate Traits of Professional Learning

Developing appropriate professional learning activities to perfect teaching and develop the skills of instructional leaders is an infinite process. As educators, we should constantly be changing what we are doing, researching what is working, and modifying our practice accordingly. Our craft should be a constant study—a constant internal questioning of our methodologies. Some refer to this as "lifelong learning," but too many people interpret that phrase as continuing their own education by taking courses in isolation from their colleagues. Twenty-first-century learning on the part of our students demands that all educators engage in this continuous improvement. However, twenty-first-century learning requires some specifics that differ from our current practice.

Just as teachers are expected to address standards and indicators in teaching students, principals have to consider the standards that have been established for professional learning. The National Staff Development Council (2010) has identified excellent standards for professional learning that principals should be familiar with. Sending teachers to workshops, conferences, or sessions during district in-service days to attend "dog and pony shows" about any new concepts that have no relevance to a longitudinal learning plan for teachers is not going to work. The research clearly indicates that simply sitting in a conference and listening to theory will not change behavior for the majority of us. That's not to say that there isn't a place for stand-alone presentations on particular topics. Having a speaker on a particular topic can be appropriate to motivate faculty, to introduce a long-term training plan, to wrap up a long-term training plan, and so on. However, "sit and get" workshops should always tie into a larger improvement plan. Teachers have to know that what they're hearing has an impact on what they're going to be doing in their classrooms in the very near future.

Let's think about adults as learners. In order to create a classroom environment where students are eagerly engaged in being prepared for work and college, we're going to have to change the way teachers think about teaching. Knowles (1980) offers four principles for andragogy (adult learning): Adults need to be involved in the planning and evaluation of their instruction; experience (including mistakes) provides the basis for learning activities; adults are most interested in learning subjects that have immediate relevance to their job or personal life; adult learning is problem-centered rather than content-oriented (ironically, these four principles are very close to the authors' earlier definition of twenty-first-century learning).

In addition, professional learning should be ongoing in order for the majority of teachers to change what they are doing in the classroom. Teachers have to be involved in learning communities with their peers, studying problems that pertain to the students that they are currently teaching. Being engaged with colleagues and sharing ideas and strategies that apply to what they use in the classroom the very next day is what will change teaching

Reflecting . . .

It is said that if you know your enemies and know yourself, you will not be imperiled in a hundred battles; if you do not know your enemies but do know yourself, you will win one and lose one; if you do not know your enemies nor yourself, you will be imperiled in every single battle.

—Sun Tzu, *The Art of War*

Obviously, we should know ourselves and our students, but who or what is the enemy?

behaviors over time. Professional learning communities, when implemented appropriately, usually have successfully addressed these needs. Of course, teachers need to be led through the collaborative process by a skilled facilitator using relevant and scientifically based research, or the exercise is simply shared ignorance.

The design of professional training is crucial to the outcome. According to Killion (2008), 5 to 10 percent of teachers will use their new learning when professional learning consists of mere presentation of theory; 10 to 15 percent will use their new learning when demonstration and low-risk practice are added; and 85 to 90 percent will use their new learning when ongoing supports in the forms of coaching and study groups are added.

Even after teachers have been through a successful professional learning experience where they have come to understand that there is a need for change in their classrooms, that first step in initiating an instructional change can still be quite intimidating for both teachers and principals. Teachers and principals alike need to be curious and adventurous about implementing new strategies, but that doesn't mean they need to be reckless or overreaching. When trying anything new, it is always best to start with small steps with the intention of creating a snowball effect.

Thinking back to the traits of career center classes, described earlier, which of those traits could you first replicate at your school with ease through a professional learning activity if your teachers indicated such a need? For example, if you're working in a school where math scores are weak and your teachers have indicated they want more training on incorporating collaborative lessons in order to improve student achievement, how would you do it? Let's get even more focused—how can you ensure that your math classrooms become more collaborative? Or even more focused—how can you make one lesson in one classroom more collaborative in nature than it was before?

Start with one teacher—say, your sixth-grade math teacher, Ms. ZZZ. Ms. ZZZ is willing to take a step in making her lessons more collaborative. She also has some leadership potential and influence over other teachers in her grade level and department. Pick a standard that she is going to be teaching in the near future and sit down with her and write a lesson together (think about what a powerful message that will send to your faculty and staff when

Reflecting . . .

> Teachers clearly dislike the "sit and get" types of professional learning they typically receive during faculty meetings, yet that's exactly how they design most of their classes. Why is that?

you model planning together). You have to walk into the situation knowing *and acknowledging* that Ms. ZZZ is likely to know more about math than you do, but you also have to communicate that the purpose of your meeting is to make the delivery of the content more collaborative for the students.

Ms. ZZZ will soon be teaching the following Common Core State Standard: "Fluently divide multi-digit numbers using the standard algorithm" (6.NS). (You could also address several Listening and Speaking standards with this lesson as well). It should go without saying that she is going to address this standard with her class because she has determined that at least 80 percent of her students have not already mastered it. During your meeting, talk about conventional ways that she would normally address this standard and then discuss ideas to make the lesson more collaborative in just *one* of her classes. Talk about the specific class and have Ms. ZZZ set a time limit on group work if her students aren't used to working in collaborative groups. For example, she may want to start with a five-minute activity (she may also need to go over group norms with the class and practice those a bit before breaking the class into groups for instructional purposes).

Here are a few ideas to get you thinking or to serve as discussion starters with a leadership team:

A lesson in using no technology:

The teacher introduces the standard and provides a few examples (ten minutes). The information and examples remain on an anchor chart or the board throughout the lesson. Students are divided into groups of four to work on several problems the teacher has created (fifteen minutes). The groups then report their answers and how they derived those answers to the rest of the class (twenty minutes). The teacher then reviews the concept, referring to the introductory part of the lesson.

Depending on the level of understanding of the students, the teacher can tweak this lesson by having students develop word problems for other groups in the class—which could ultimately become the real assessment of the standard after the teacher reviews the questions for content.

A lesson in using technology:

For homework, have students watch a lesson on a specific standard at the Kahn Academy website (2011). Review the lesson at the start of class (five minutes). In small groups, have students create a slideshow of five problems and their solutions that require using online resources. We encourage you to consider the SCALE UP criteria for groups (Beichner 2010), which, although developed with college students, can be easily adapted to K–12 environments.

Have students submit the presentations to you online for review (five minutes). Share your own slide show of problems to the class for review (five minutes).

The good news is that if you're struggling to change the culture of your school to make more of your classrooms look like the classes described, or if you're finding it difficult to think of good examples to use with the grade levels and/or subjects in your particular education setting, help is on the way!

The CCSI suggests many of the faulty learning characteristics that exist in schools today should be replaced by characteristics described in twenty-first-century learning. Previously, the authors indicated that thinking, working in teams, and using other soft skills were traits of twenty-first-century learning. What will it take for teachers to begin acquiring these skills?

Addressing Marginal Teacher Performance

Teachers whose performance is marginal will require close monitoring and specifically designed professional learning to address their needs. While procedures will differ from district to district and even from state to state, there is no question that in the profession, there is an expectation that even marginal teachers deserve the opportunity to improve. We encourage you to ensure that you know the legal rights of teachers and the responsibilities of administrators in addressing marginal performance in your district and state. As the focus of this book is on leading learning, professional learning for teachers, regardless of where they are today, is critical.

Strategies for improving performance start with clear evidence of a teacher's current level of performance. Throughout this book, the authors have often said "see Chapter 4." Why? Because everything you do must start with data. In determining the professional learning needs of teachers, data sources should include student test scores (standardized and teacher-made tests), grades, attendance, discipline referrals, classroom observations of teaching and learning, and so on. While the individual teacher data is important, you will also need comparative data. For example, let's consider discipline referrals. To assess whether a teacher needs professional learning in managing students, you need the individual teacher's referrals (type, frequency, students involved), comparative data (how often the referred students are referred from other teachers for similar behaviors), and a clear understanding of the school's policies on student conduct. Remember, if you collect the data, use it!

Since the range of needs of teachers whose performance is marginal is varied, it would take a whole book to identify appropriate actions that the principal could take and professional learning opportunities specific to the needs of the teachers. Suffice it to say that if you use the data to identify the teachers' needs, design professional learning to address those needs, and provide support and monitoring for the teachers, you will hopefully help them improve in creating productive student learning. Should a teacher fail to improve, however, you will have the evidence you need (remember, Chapter 4!) to use your district and state procedures for moving that teacher out of the teaching ranks.

Parents and Community

Topics for professional learning extend beyond instruction. Over many years of observing what principals and superintendents do, the authors have concluded that superintendents spend more time on public relations with parents and community than principals do. However, principals can find that they spend a great deal of time managing the needs and interests of parents and the community. Yet, interestingly, there is relatively little professional learning available for teachers or principals on issues revolving around community norms.

As an elementary principal, you know that safety is a serious concern for parents. No principal or teacher wants a child to be hurt. Parents certainly do not want their children hurt. Playgrounds are notoriously arenas where accidents occur. No matter how many adults are on playground duty, they can't see every child and every inch of the ground at every minute. Usually, teachers will cluster in groups talking to each other while, perhaps, periodically scanning the playground. It is only natural that teachers, isolated from their peers while in their classrooms and responsible for student learning, want the opportunity to talk to each other. And people are so socialized to look at each other when they talk that it is difficult for teachers not to do so. Principals can address both the students' need for safety and the faculty's need for social contact by teaching teachers how to have a conversation without looking at each other. During faculty meetings, ask teachers to stand in a half circle, facing out and talking to each other without turning their heads to look at each other. At first it will seem silly, then awkward, but ultimately the teachers will find that they can meet their professional responsibilities to monitor students on the playground and satisfy their personal needs for adult interaction at the same time. (This is a much better solution than demanding that teachers stand separately from each other at specific locations on the playground, an alternative that would undoubtedly raise a rebellion).

The topics that may need to be addressed to serve the needs of parents and the community will be as varied as the location of each school. Both teachers and principals may be challenged when conferencing with same-gender parents, poorly educated parents, highly educated parents, divorced parents, and bullying parents. Principals also have to deal with the expectations of community leaders.

More and more students come from blended or single-parent families. Current data show that less than 30 percent of children and young people live in what is perceived as the "traditional" family (two parents with their biological children). Many teachers operate from an assumption that the traditional family is the norm and that there is something wrong for students who do not live in that circumstance. But a student's home situation is not ours to judge in the school setting. Teachers should stay focused on the student's performance and not on any family situation that may be perceived as the "cause" of behavior problems. A teacher does not have to approve of a family's lifestyle, but in the school setting, the only thing that matters is the student's performance and learning.

Parents bring their stressors into the school just as their children do. We choose to believe that old adage, "Parents send us the best children they have." From May to August 1992, due to dramatic economic shifts in the community, the population of the school where Jacque was principal went from 9 percent minority and 18 percent receiving free or reduced-cost lunch to 62 percent minority and 83 percent receiving free or reduced-cost lunch. A well-intentioned teacher said, "What are we going to do? We don't know how to teach these kids?" Jacque said, "What do you mean by 'these kids'?" The teacher said, "Poor kids." To which Jacque replied, without even realizing how strongly she felt about it, "Children do not choose the circumstances into which they were born, nor in which they live. We must teach each one." That led them to a very meaningful discussion of how to teach students who might not have had the opportunities outside of school of prior clientele and also help their parents feel comfortable in the school and the community. They ultimately devised learning opportunities for teachers to work with parents that benefited the entire school community: teacher-led sessions on the "typical" performance of students in each grade; getting a grant to provide computers for parents to use at home if they came to school for training and committed to working with their children on homework; establishing evening media-center hours by changing the media specialist's work hours to 12–8 instead of 8–4; and getting the public library to extend its mobile library services to include evenings at our school so parents could access library resources.

The authors include this example not to provide a "cure" for dealing with poverty, but to help you think about all the possibilities that could be solutions in your school when you "think differently" and prepare teachers to do the same.

Another example deals with parents who behave as bullies. As principal, Jacque told her teachers that none of them had to take abuse from anyone. She set up practice sessions with teachers on how to handle situations with parents who were being overly aggressive, if not bullying. The first thing they practiced saying was, "Mr. X, I sense that you are upset at the moment and I really want to talk with you about your daughter, Sue. So while I go get something I need from the teacher workroom, please write down two or three things you would like us to accomplish in this meeting." Then the teacher leaves the room (if the teacher has no real destination, he or she can go get a blank folder from another room). Some teachers have said, "Well, what if he tears up my room?" Jacque's response was, "Then I'll deal with that. But you don't have to sit there and let him yell at you." Generally, by helping the parents focus on the outcomes they desired for the meeting, the teacher can help them calm down. If this strategy does not work, the teacher should say, "Mr. X, I don't think we will be able to solve this problem together, so I'm leaving now and going to the office and asking the principal to meet with us. You are welcome to come with me." Jacque assured the teachers that they had "permission" (some need the principal to say that) to come to the office or call for her. The point of this example is that some professional learning requires little time to develop, but does require observation on your part to see the need. Parents and community members are as interested in the work educators do as they are. Our students are their children and the future success of their communities. Forge those partnerships.

In working with parents, it is always important to remember that we do not know what the student has learned from us or from them. It is clearly possible and likely that a student learns much outside of school. However, we are responsible for assessing the student's performance in the school environment and we need to help parents and community members to know and understand that.

Wrapping It Up

You do not have to be the one to present every professional learning opportunity and the authors don't think you should. You need to be a learner just as you expect your teachers to be. We have frequently heard teachers express frustration that they have to sit through professional learning when no administrator is there to learn what they've been taught or will ever know if they use what was presented. Please do not be one of those administrators, because if you are you will not be a *leader* of learning.

Professional learning must move from something done *to* teachers to something done *for* the improvement of student engagement in learning. Whether the focus is increasing content knowledge, instructional strategies, assessment, or group work, all professional learning must begin with a focus on the intended outcomes: implementation and assessment. Are you set to ensure that such outcomes are identified and monitored?

USING WHAT YOU'VE LEARNED

The process you are about to read should be spread out over several meetings or online sessions so teachers have time to process and reflect on the information they are producing and/or receiving. For these activities, teachers should be randomly assigned to groups (this helps keep the discussion objective and focused on schoolwide issues as opposed to grade-level or department issues) and not allowed to sit with their friends. Have each group designate a speaker, but also provide all teachers with two colors of index cards to provide written feedback (one color for group responses, the other for individual responses). Explain that teachers will have the opportunity to submit their thoughts independently and anonymously on the index cards, which will be collected.

Step 1: State the purpose of the meeting—for example, "To ensure a clear vision of how our school's professional learning activities work to assist teachers meet state and federal requirements for meeting the learning needs of students, and to define our own expectations for student achievement."

Step 2: State the essential questions for the meeting. The following are some examples:

1. As an educator, what is your ultimate job?
2. What role do academic standards play in your job?
3. What roles do formative and summative assessments play in your job?
4. What professional learning activities are we using that assist you?
5. Do we need to change or drop any instructional or professional learning practices that are inefficient or ineffective?

Step 3: Walk the teachers through each of the essential questions that you've given them. The following is an example of the process:

Provide teachers with the following question, "As an educator, what is your ultimate job?" Ask them to discuss this in their group for two minutes and write a summary on an index card. Teachers should also write their independent thoughts on index cards if they desire. Randomly ask groups to summarize their responses, but collect all the index cards.

Step 4: After each question, collect the index cards in such a way that the teachers know they will remain anonymous. (One way to do this is to turn the cards upside down as you take them and shuffle them as you move around.) After the session, have each response typed into one document, sort the responses based on similarity, and then report all the responses back to the entire group. Note which responses came from a group and which were individual responses. Based on the majority of responses to each question, the principal (or better yet, a school leadership team) can make recommendations for professional learning activities for the school.

If the summary of responses doesn't provide any clear answers for "next steps" in professional learning, the principal (and other appropriate instructional leaders) may take a day to visit teachers in teams, such as grade levels or departments, during planning times to gather clarifying information.

What does this activity accomplish? Have you provided each teacher with a voice in the decision-making process? Is the culmination of ideas a true reflection of what the teachers believe as a group? Can teachers objectively place blame with the principal for the decisions made?

7

Personal Best

As educators, we have all studied Maslow's (1943) hierarchy of basic needs. Interestingly, when educators talk about this hierarchy, they almost always think about it in relation to the students they serve. Hungry children (physiological needs) find it difficult to learn, so our society has developed a system of providing free or reduced-cost lunches. Children who live in fear, either of their home environments, community, or yes, sadly, even their classroom or school, are challenged to learn because their need for safety isn't being met. Thus, we have rules and policies to ensure a safe learning environment for our students. Students' social needs are being met in ways today that most teachers never imagined. Even elementary-school children have cell phones today, and although they are likely to comply with school rules about the use of the cell phones, their high-school counterparts are texting underneath their desks. Many students even have smartphones allowing them to do searches for information right at the moment of trying to answer a question. These technological innovations seem to be clear evidence of the social needs of children and young people and how they are trying to meet them. In general, most schools provide for the three most basic needs as defined by Maslow: physiological, safety, and social. And, in fact, the need for self-esteem is met for many through their performance academically or in sports, music, art, or clubs. However, we have given little attention to how to address the esteem needs of students who are failing in our defined systems. While self-actualization may not occur for many of us until we are well into adulthood, if then, it will be far less likely to occur for children and young people (defined appropriately for their age group) if their basic needs are not met. That is, their personal bests may not be realized without direct interventions. Most educators know and believe they have a role to play in the developmental needs of the students they serve. Do they know *how* to meet those needs in an educational setting?

Reflecting . . .

Does your personal best interfere with your leadership? A colleague once told Jacque that she would be a great administrator, but followed it with, "But I wouldn't want to work for you." Jacque said, "Then I wouldn't be a great administrator." He said, "Yes, you would. You are a leader, you're organized, you see the big picture, but are also good at details." Her response was, "Well, thank you for that, but why wouldn't you want to work with me?" He said, "Because you have such high expectations for yourself and I don't want to work that hard." She said, "I know I am a type A, but I don't expect that of others." He said, "It doesn't matter. People see your work ethic and feel they have to work that hard." Although we wouldn't all want to try to live up to type A personalities, this story demonstrates the influence of personal expectations.

If your personal best includes high expectations for your own performance, what impact does that have on those you are trying to lead? What systems do you have in place to gather feedback so you have a barometer of the impact of your actions on others?

The greatest good we can do for others is not just to share our riches with them, but to reveal theirs. —Zig Ziglar

Meeting the Basic Needs of Adults

If we expect teachers to give their personal best, day in and day out, there has to be a definition of what that personal best looks like.

Throughout the chapters in this book, you have been presented with things to think about, problems to consider, solutions to develop, and strategies to use in moving toward positive action. Arriving at your personal best and supporting others to reach their personal best require discussion to determine the characteristics of a personal best so that everyone knows it when they see it.

Clearly, each person's personal best is going to be different. The first-year teacher will have a different personal best than a veteran teacher of ten years. On a recent visit to Japan, Jacque visited a teacher education center that offers professional development for the region. She learned that Japan puts a strong focus on professional development throughout a teacher's career, with focused development activities at the tenth and twentieth years as a means of renewal. Do we have such a focus? Is it possible for educators in the United

States to even consider that they might need a renewal every ten years? How much difference is there between teachers in the first and twentieth years of their careers? That is, does the teacher have twenty years' experience or has he had the same experience twenty times?

The principal of a school segregated by race/ethnicity, socioeconomic status, and student test scores was concerned that many of the teachers seemed to blame the minority race students for their academic performance being below proficient. She had her teachers complete an exercise to identify the greatest needs in the school. She was disappointed and frustrated that student achievement was listed by only one team of teachers. All the rest listed such things as noise in the halls, end-of-school dismissal, and poor student attitudes. When Jacque, a district consultant, saw the results, she said, "I'm not surprised. These issues indicate that basic needs of these teachers are not being met. For some the noise is physiological discomfort, for others these problems cause them to feel unsafe, and for others the student behaviors violate their social norms." The principal just stared at her. Then she said, "Why haven't I thought of this? Why have I only considered Maslow's hierarchy related to our students?" It isn't easy to look inside one's own house. Just as teachers are integral to the learning environment in their classrooms,

Reflecting . . .

> Do the adults in your school have their basic needs met? While issues of personal privacy must be considered, principals often are called upon to support a faculty or staff member when his or her physiological needs change—though serious illness, for example. Do the teachers and staff in your school feel safe? Not just physically safe, but emotionally safe? How do you know?
>
> Schools are communities. Are the social needs of your teachers and staff met in the school community? It is not your job to entertain, but social needs can be as basic as someone saying, "How are you today? How's your family?" (and demonstrating caring about the answer).
>
> We often assume that teachers have their esteem needs met because they are professionals. But are those needs met? What evidence do you have for knowing the self-esteem of your faculty and staff?
>
> Self-actualization, while dependent on the first four levels of Maslow's hierarchy, will likely require some dialogue to determine what it looks like for a professional in your school. How would you determine a definition for self-actualization among faculty at your school?

principals are integral to the environment of their schools. It is not easy to see all the interactions or how we are perceived, and sometimes we don't even know our own needs. The good news? As educators we *are* part of a community. Although we have developed a close–the-door way of operating over the last fifty or so years, we can open those doors to the extent it is necessary to develop and nurture the community.

Privacy laws protect employees from sharing personal information that principals do not have the need to know. Don't ask! But you do have the right and responsibility to ensure a safe and orderly environment for learning. Using faculty meeting time to determine, through an activity or discussion, what would create the best environment for teachers to ensure student learning is worth the time.

As an adaptation of an activity discussed with a colleague, also a principal, one year Jacque asked the school custodian to dig a two-foot by two-foot hole next to the woods by the school property. At a faculty meeting, she gave each teacher a piece of paper with the prompt: Write down everything about our school that makes you frustrated, angry, annoyed, or just plain mad. (Some wrote furiously.) When they finally finished, she asked them to put the papers in a shoe box that she had spray-painted black. They then followed her outside to the hole. She put the box in the hole and invited each teacher to shovel dirt on it. She said nothing else. The group then walked back into the school building, where she said, "We have buried our anger, frustrations, and disappointments. Now I want you to write three things that you want to celebrate about our students and our school with a focus on things we can enhance."

The response to this activity was amazing. One teacher confessed, "I didn't realize how much I had pent up inside me. It was good to get it out and bury it." Another said, "I couldn't imagine you were going to let us dwell on the negative, but I never saw the burial coming. It was like the proverbial burying the hatchet. Made me feel good." There are times you need to know what the anger, frustrations, and disappointments are, but without a focus on the positives in your community, you will likely stay busy just trying to keep everyone afloat at the very basic levels of need.

Adults who can work toward or achieve the level of self-actualization are much more likely to be prepared to focus on the needs of their students and figure out ways to ensure their learning success. The role of a school leader is helping the teachers and staff achieve their personal best through meeting their basic needs (or helping them find help to do so) and enhancing their esteem and steps toward self-actualization.

Focusing on Students versus Adults

While this heading may seem to contradict the earlier material in this chapter, it is the authors' opinion that we have to change the focus of schools back to the students. Over the last half of the twentieth century and yes, even into the first decade of the twenty-first, the focus of education seems to have become the adults. Schools are about students. Students in K–12 are young people in their developmental years. They are not mini-adults, as hard as that is for some teachers to accept. If the focus in your school—every decision—was predicated on what's right for your students, would your students behave academically and socially differently than they do now? How would you know?

Creating an expectation among teachers and students that students will know and be able to articulate their learning, across multiple settings, puts the focus on the students. One kindergarten teacher created frustration for her peers because she required each student to give her a piece of knowledge or information from their morning work before they entered the cafeteria. This, of course, took time and caused others to wait in the hall. The principal, aware of the frustration of the other teachers, took some time to think about how to address it. Then she said, "I've observed the strategy you use to have students draw on their learning from the morning and I think it is a great idea. I've also noted that implementing it at the door to the cafeteria delays other students who want to get their lunch. Do you have some ideas about how you could keep the strategy and not cause others to be late?" With almost no hesitation, the teacher said, "I'd be happy to have my class lunch last or I could switch to having the kids tell me before they line up. What do you think?" Since kindergartners ate last in that school, the principal simply changed this class to the last lunch and everyone's needs were met—a simple fix to meeting the adult needs while focusing on the students' learning activity.

The principal must ensure that all adults in the school have a focus on student learning. Your actions and words model for others that you hold yourself accountable for the expectations. Students will be challenged to

Reflecting . . .

> Many schools have student work posted in hallways and classrooms. Many teachers even post rubrics that explain the assessment of the work. But who decides what goes on the walls? The teacher? Or the students? Whom does the posted work help? In two elementary schools the authors visited recently, the student work was at adult eye level. How does that help the students?

do their best if the adults in the building have high expectations for students and give them the tools to reach those expectations. As shown by the example in Chapter 4 of Mrs. D, the esteemed social studies teacher, students are capable of understanding what is expected of them if the adults provide the opportunity. When graduate students in education state that seeing a rubric in their graduate classes was the first time they truly knew what was expected of them, we have to question what we are doing: Do as I say, not as I do?

Teachers and administrators can no more get into our student's brains than they can into ours. All we know about our students is what they say and what they do. The same is true for the adults. If the adults in a school respond to every situation by focusing on its effect on their needs as adults rather than on what students need, there's lots of work to be done.

Wrapping It Up

Over the years, regardless of the positions the authors have held, they have both made a conscious effort to thank teachers, individually and collectively, for the work they do every day. Teaching is important work. Learning is more important.

As educators, we are extremely fortunate to have lots of "new beginnings": new school years, new semesters, new kids, and, yes, new teachers. But most of all we are fortunate to have a profession that allows us to make a positive difference for children and young people every day. We can't lose sight of that opportunity. As a leader in your school, you can either rise to the occasion or you can shut your door.

Ms. Jan King, North Carolina's Principal of the Year in 2010, is highly respected and revered by her students, teachers, and community. She unabashedly states, "Teachers know that I have nonnegotiables and the one that they can all state is that students come first. In all things." To accomplish this goal, she expects that every question, concern, idea, and strategy is addressed by first considering what it means for each student. If there is money to be spent, she asks how it will help students learn. If someone wants to change the schedule, she expects the proposal to include how the change will help students learn. Ms. King clearly states and supports her expectations for faculty, staff, students, and the school community.

If our expectations for ourselves include doing and being our personal best, we can help others to let their lights shine through their personal best.

Reflecting . . .

A principal set three expectations for teachers at the beginning of the year: they should adhere to the teacher dress code, they should not give zeros for homework, and they should document three minor infractions with parental contact before a student could be referred to the principal for minor infractions. He was dismayed that a significant percentage of teachers were not following these rules.

At the next faculty meeting, he asked, "Why do you think some students don't follow the rules?" As the teachers brainstormed, he recorded their responses on chart paper: poor parenting, recalcitrant, stubborn, don't care, want control, power struggle. Then he asked, "Why do you think some teachers don't follow the rules?" A stunned hush fell over the room. Then the teacher he viewed as the biggest offender shouted out, "Well, I didn't agree to your rules in the first place." The principal walked over to the chart paper and circled "power struggle." Then he said, "And we're not going to have one of these" and left the room.

The principal didn't sleep well that night and almost dreaded returning to school the next morning. But, much to his surprise, he had many e-mails and even some notes under his door thanking him. One teacher wrote, "Thank you for holding us ALL to the rules." Another said, "I'm sorry I have not set an example of following rules for my students because I haven't followed the rules set for me. If I object to the rules, I should have discussed my point of view with you."

Would you have the courage to do this?

USING WHAT YOU'VE LEARNED

Ask three people you respect and trust (a teacher, colleague, friend, spouse, etc.) to give you the answers to three questions:

1. What do you see as the best thing(s) I do as a person?
2. What do you see as the best thing(s) I do as a principal?
3. Tell me something I can do to improve one aspect of my role as principal in order to be a better leader of learning.

Then read and think about what they tell you. You can grow from hearing the positive things people have to say about you, and you can grow from their observations, too.

Conclusion

The authors hope that you have found value in thinking through the ideas and materials in this book. It has been our goal to provide principals, those studying to be principals, and leaders of all learning, regardless of position or title, with different examples, activities, and questions to guide their thinking and actions regarding changes that need to occur in the learning environments of K–12 schools. It is only through consideration of yourselves as learners and through your actions that we can hope to bring about positive change for students. We have every confidence that you *are* leaders of learning.

References

Anderson, L. W., Krathwohl, D. R., & Bloom, B. S. (2001). *A taxonomy for learning, teaching, and assessing: A revision of Bloom's taxonomy of educational objectives.* New York: Longman.

Beichner, R. (2010). *Student-Centered Active Learning Environment for Undergraduate Programs: SCALE UP.* Retrieved from http://scaleup.ncsu.edu/.

Berry, W. (2010). *GoodReads.* Retrieved from http://www.goodreads.com/quotes/search?q=It+may+be+when+we+no+longer+know+what+to+do&commit=Search.

Buskey, F. H. (Program Director). (2010). MSA Mantra. Cullowhee, NC: Western Carolina University.

Carlyle, T. ([1833] 2000). *Sartor Resartus.* In S. Kreis, *Lectures on modern European intellectual history. The History Guide.* Retrieved from http://www.historyguide.org/intellect/press.html.

CCSSI. (2011). *Common Core State Standards Initiative.* Retrieved from http://www.corestandards.org/the-standards/english-language-arts-standards/anchor-standards-hssts/college-and-career-readiness-anchor-standards-for-writing/.

Clifford, P., & Friesen, S. (2007). Creating essential questions. Retrieved from http://www.galileo.org/tips/essential_questions.html.

The Critical Thinking Community. (2010). Retrieved from http://www.criticalthinking.org/pages/defining-critical-thinking/766.

Gibson, R., Toffler, A., & Toffler, H. (1998). *Rethinking the future: Rethinking business, principles, competition, control and complexity, eadership, markets, and the world.* Boston: Nicholas Brealey.

Glazier, R. (2011, March). *Bold leadership in challenging times.* Keynote address presented at the North Carolina Association for School Administrators state conference, Raleigh, NC.

Glickman, C., Gordon, S. P., & Ross-Gordon, J. M. (2004). *Supervision and instructional leadership: A developmental approach.* Boston: Allyn and Bacon.

Goertz, M. E., Floden, R. E., & O'Day, J. (1995). *Studies of educational reform: Systemic reform.* New Brunswick, NJ: Consortium for Policy Research in Education.

Hebert, E. A. (1999). Rugtime for teachers: Reinventing the faculty meeting. *Phi Delta Kappan, 81*(3), 219–222.

Henein, A., & Morissette, F. (2007). *Made in Canada leadership: Wisdom from the nation's best and brightest on leadership practice and development.* Mississauga, ON: John Wiley.

Herzog, H. (2010). *Some We Love, Some We Hate, Some We Eat: Why It's So Hard to Think Straight About Animals.* New York: HarperCollins.

Hindo, B. (2007, June 11). At 3M, a struggle between efficiency and creativity. *BusinessWeek, 4038,* 8–14.

Human Synergistics Lab. (2011). Life Styles Inventory (LSI 1 & 2). Retrieved from http://www.humansynergistics.com/products/lsi.aspx.

Jacobs, H. H. (2010). *Curriculum 21: Essential education for a changing world.* Alexandria, VA: ASCD.

Jacobs, J. E., & Rotholz, J. N. (2005). *Leading learning in a changing world: Using children's literature for professional dialogue*. Latham, MD: Scarecrow Press.

Jacobs, M. (2010). *Personal posting in University Course Education Leadership 714.* The role of school leaders in special education, Western Carolina University, Cullowhee, NC (used with permission).

Kahn Academy. (2011). *Multiplication 6: Multiple digit numbers: Working our way up to multiplying multi-digit numbers*. Retrieved from http://www.khanacademy.org/video/multiplication-6-multiple-digit-numbers?playlist=Arithmetic.

Kawasaki, G. (2007). *Creating a mantra*. Retrieved from http://www.youtube.com/watch?v=4q6_ARD6c_g.

Killion, J. (2008). *Assessing impact: Evaluating staff development* (2nd ed.). Thousand Oaks, CA: Corwin Press.

Knowles, M. (1980). *The modern practice of adult education: Andragogy versus pedagogy*. Englewood Cliffs, NJ: Prentice Hall/Cambridge.

Kreis, S. (2000). Lectures on modern European intellectual history. *The History Guide*. Retrieved from http://www.hisotryguide.org/intellect/press.html.

Leadership Compass. (2011). Retrieved from http://www.bonner.org.

Lee, B., Little, J., Logan, B. (2000). *Bruce Lee: A warrior's journey* (Motion picture). Warner Home Video.

Maslow, A. (1943). A theory of human motivation. *Psychological Review, 50*, 370–396.

Mayfield, P. (2010). *Building trust in the workplace*. Retrieved from http://hotjobs.yahoo.com/career-articles-6_steps_to_building_trust_in_the_workplace-548.

McKissick, P. (2000). *The honest to goodness truth*. New York: Simon & Schuster.

Mizell, M. H. (2002). *Shooting for the sun: The message of middle school reform*. New York: Edna M. Clark Foundation.

MLQ30 management & leadership test. (2011). Retrieved from http://www.myskillsprofile:global.

National Staff Development Council Standards. (2010). Retrieved from http://www.learningforward.org/standards/index.cfm.

North Carolina Department of Public Instruction (NCDPI). (2010). Teacher working conditions survey. Retrieved from http://www.ncteachingconditions.org/.

The Partnership for 21st Century Skills. (2010). Critical thinking and problem solving. Retrieved from http://www.p21.org/component/content/article/260.

Patterson, K., Grenny, J., Maxfield, D., McMillan, R., & Switzler, A. (2008). *Influencer: The power to change anything*. New York: McGraw Hill.

Reeves, D. (2010). *Leaders embracing the data teams process: Leadership and learning live*, volume 3, DVD 3. Englewood, CO: The Leadership and Learning Center.

Rhodes, L. A. (2003). *The profound knowledge school*. Retrieved from http://education.jhu.edu/newhorizons/Transforming%20Education/Articles/The%20Profound%20Knowledge%20School/index.html.

Smart-Survey.com. (2011) Retrieved from http://www.smart-survey.co.uk/.

Socrates. (n.d). BrainyQuote. Retrieved from http://www.brainyquote.com/quotes/authors/s/socrates.html.

Stevenson, K. (2010). *Educational trends shaping school planning, design, construction, funding, and operation*. Retrieved from http://www.ncef.org/pubs/educationaltrends.pdf.

Stronge, J. H. (2002). *Qualities of effective teachers*. Alexandria, VA: ASCD.

Sun Tzu. (2009). *The Art of War*. London: Penguin Classics.
SurveyMonkey. (2010). Retrieved from http://try.surveymonkey.com/?gclid=CJCR-dPg8qsCFZFV7Aod6noeMw.
Toffler, A. (1998). Foreword. In R. Gibson, A. Toffler, & H. Toffler, *Rethinking the future: Rethinking business, principles, competition, control & complexity, leadership, markets, and the world*. Boston, MA: Nicholas Brealey.
US Department of Education. (2010). *No child left behind*. Retrieved from http://www2.ed.gov/nclb/landing.jhtml.
Vatterott, C. (2010). Five hallmarks of good homework. *Educational Leadership*, 68(1), 10–15.
Wikipedia. (2011). *Problem-based learning*. Retrieved from http://en.wikipedia.org/wiki/Problem-based_learning.
Wagner, T. (2008). *The global achievement gap: Why even our best schools don't teach the new survival skills our children need—and what we can do about it*. New York: Basic Books.
Wagner, T. (2010). Video talk. Retrieved from http://www.schoolchange.org.
York-Barr, J., Sommerness, J., & Hur, J. (2008). Teacher leadership: Leading from the middle . . . learning side-by-side. In T. Good, *21st century education: A reference handbook*. Thousand Oaks, CA: Sage.
Zepeda, S. J. (2012). *Professional development: What works* (2nd ed.). Larchmont, NY: Eye On Education.
Ziglar, Zig. (2011). *7 Powerful and Amazingly Motivational Quotes from Zig Ziglar*. Retrieved from http://www.dumblittleman.com/2010/10/7-powerful-and-amazingly-motivational.html.
Zoomerang. (2010). Retrieved from http://www.zoomerang.com.

Notes

Notes

Notes